Sowing and Reaping: You Can't Harvest What You Are Unwilling to Plant

Dr. Jason Pfledderer

Cover design by: K&T Graphics

Edited by: Eve Editing Services

Disclaimer

A cardinal rule of Biblical interpretation, as in the case of the interpretation of any written document, is always **"context rules."**

My job as a Biblical expositor is always to determine the meaning that the original Biblical author—and ultimately God Himself—intended a passage to mean. Therefore, I use the acronym S.T.O.P as a guideline for Biblical interpretation:

Situation — What is the situation in this passage? Read the passage for context. What is the specific <u>situation</u> in this passage?

Type of literature — Is this passage poetry, narrative, prophetic, or apocalyptic? Different types of literature have different rules of interpretation. Poetry and prophetic writing, for example, contain many figures of speech that are not to be interpreted literally but figuratively. Isaiah 13 is a good example:

> *Behold, the day of the Lord comes, cruel, with*
> *wrath and fierce anger, to make the land a*
> *desolation and to destroy its sinners from it. For*
> *the stars of the heavens and their constellations*
> *will not give their light; the sun will be dark at*
> *its rising, and the moon will not shed its light.*

This is prophetic hyperbole. God often uses cosmic deconstruction language in passages foretelling judgment upon a nation as in this passage prophesying judgment on

Babylon. The same language occurs again later when God foretold judgment upon Egypt. Jesus used the same imagery in Matthew's Gospel when he described the impending judgment on the covenant people of Israel that was fulfilled in the destruction of Jerusalem in 70 AD. Failure to appreciate such phenomena of language has led to all kinds of heresy and even the establishment of many religious cults.

Object of the passage — What is the object of this passage? What is the point the author is making? Again, context must determine what the <u>object</u> of the passage is.

Prescriptive or descriptive — Not every passage is prescriptive. Much Biblical narrative is telling a story of what happened in a particular instance, and there is no indication in the text that a general prescription is being made. A good example is the story of Elijah dousing the wood. He was a prophet of God and his story is not a model of what every New Testament Christian should be doing today!

I give you this guide to help you consider Scripture and not to ignore context. Context is always the key in Biblical interpretation; otherwise, an individual is using God's Word unethically and can make it just about mean anything they desire. Therefore, I would like to make this disclaimer:

With the vast array of denominations and the large numbers of theologians, there are a myriad of opinions on Biblical topics. Knowing this, I have made every effort to line up the contents of this book as closely as possible with Scripture. I hope that you enjoy it!

Acknowledgements

God has blessed me beyond reason throughout my life. Not only has He given me the Holy Spirit who aims me in the right direction but also surrounds me with the most perfect examples of intelligence, wisdom, and strength. I give all the glory to God first and those who lead me to His understanding second.

My leadership is not something I can boast about. God and His people have bestowed upon me much knowledge. The reason I can see so far is not only due to my own vision but also from the great teachers, friends, mentors, and colleagues whose shoulders I have stood upon throughout my life. After years of being led by them, I am just now beginning to redistribute this information to you.

I'd like to first thank the Holy Spirit for even speaking to me and to God the Father for sending His Son Jesus Christ to pay the penalty for my sins and not giving me the punishment that I so rightfully deserve.

I would like to specifically thank Dr. Mark Lantz, my friend and mentor, for his study notes (which were used with permission) and for his unconditional love and daily encouragement. His leadership is the reason that I even entertained the thought of writing this book. He is the example who showed me how to lead others. For that and so much more, I thank you and love you deeply, brother.

Next, I'd like to say thank you to my loving wife Yankho for accepting me just the way I am and for always believing in me.

To C.L. for befriending me for the long term, helping me put my ideas into a usable format, and taking my projects to the next level.

To Professor Roger Krynock for keeping me "theologically correct."

To Emma for finally making sure it all "flows" without a hitch.

And finally, to Natasha for putting my vision into picture form.

Without all of you, this and many other projects wouldn't have been made possible. May God bless you all.

Table of Contents

Introduction

Think back to when you were a child. What was your favorite way to learn? If you were like me, it was in a way that did not feel like learning. It was a way that was fun and entertaining. In junior and senior high school, I learned about teamwork and hand-eye coordination through athletics, not even knowing I was learning it. When I got my first paper route, that was when I learned the principles of finance and responsibility without even understanding that was what was happening. And when I was very young, I began to learn many of the basic principles and lessons of God through the stories taught to me in Sunday School. It was a story time at that age and a little more. Yet, what I realized when I got older was that through these stories I was learning who God was, how He loved me, and how I was to love Him and other people. All of that was absorbed without even realizing it.

That is what is so great about the parables of Jesus. They are wonderfully insightful lessons that lead us towards being what we need to be for God, all the while not feeling like it is a task. Put plainly, the parables – *the stories of the Lord* – are fun and educational at the same time. We can learn His lessons without feeling like we are being preached to, which is why I wanted to create this book; I am desperate to be a faithful disciple maker for Christ.

This is not one of those books that break down each of the Lord's stories, pulling purpose out of each. No, the purpose of *Sowing and Reaping* is either to remind you of your role for God or to introduce you to it while urging you to value the greatest stories ever told – the parables of Jesus.

You see, the parables of Jesus hide incredible truths for the people of God. They help reveal how we are to represent the Lord Jesus Christ, how we are to be disciple makers for His Kingdom. This means knowing who He is, what He does, and why He does it, which can be extrapolated from His parables in the Gospels.

Why does Jesus teach us through parables? Let's take an in-depth look at the parable found in Matthew 13:10-13 as Jesus explains why he uses them:

Then the disciples came and said to him, "Why do you speak to them in parables?" And he answered them, "To you it has been given to know the secrets of the kingdom of heaven, but to them it has not been given. For to the one who has, more will be given, and he will have an abundance, but from the one who has not, even what he has will be taken away. <u>This is why I speak to them in parables</u>, because seeing they do not see, and hearing they do not hear, nor do they understand."

Jesus said that it was not <u>given</u> to them to understand. He was saying, "If I keep speaking clear truth, they will understand. If I speak in parables, they won't." What was the reason why Jesus taught in parables? It was a *judgment* upon their unbelief.

Speaking in parables, then, was a judgment on a willful, hard-hearted unbelief. Many of the parables Jesus used "conceal" a truth, but the reason for concealing was Jesus' judgment on the covenant breakers in Israel. This reflects what God told Isaiah. When God told Isaiah to preach judgment on the covenant breakers in Israel in his day, this is what God told him:

> *You will indeed hear but never understand, and*
> *you will indeed see but never perceive. For this*
> *people's heart has grown dull, and with their*
> *ears they can barely hear, and their eyes they*
> *have closed, lest they should see with their eyes*
> *and hear with their ears and understand with*
> *their heart and turn, and I would heal them.*

A primary reason that Jesus shifted to telling parables, as revealed by Matthew, was not just to conceal the truth, but to conceal the truth *as judgment* on the unbelief of those who rejected his clear teaching. This is why it's so important to study the entire word of God in context, so that we can understand the true meaning of what has been written.

So, I hope you dig into this book and you delight in all of His stories. I pray that you make learning about the Lord fun again. This can be accomplished by simply spending time with Him and understanding the true meaning of the parables in His word.

CHAPTER ONE

My Intention

Let us get right to the point. My intention is to help you unlock the mysteries of the Kingdom of God through explanations of the parables of Jesus. As a follower of Christ and student of His ways, you must recognize that these parables from the Lord hide incredible truths for all of us, truths that, when learned, can reveal how we are to represent the Lord Jesus Christ.

His parables are meant for you and me. I pray that you recognize this truth. He sent out these valuable teachings so that every believer that ever came along would hear them. And by hearing them, gain a level of maturity and spiritual instruction about the Kingdom of God that would produce faithful followers of Jesus that would lead the fight for goodness all the way up to the end of days.

The Bible and all that is in it is a study guide for us. It is a study guide which can instruct us how to live, learn, and teach others about Him and His ways.

When Christ ascended from this world, His parables (and the rest of Scripture) were left behind to instruct all those that He did not get to teach face to face.

MY INTENTION

My intention is to revisit Christ's parables (surely you have had an introduction to many, if not all, of them in your walk) in an effort to illuminate and answer a very important question: how does Jesus want you to live as a faithful disciple maker for His Kingdom?

CHAPTER TWO

You Are An...

As a follower of Christ, you are to be faithful to Christ.

Paul and the other apostles were serving Jesus Christ as faithful followers speaking with Christ's authority in every effort to lead unbelieving people into the right relationship with God.

As followers of Christ, we too should be faithful to our Lord in proclaiming the truth of the gospel message.

We can do this by bringing His gospel message as representatives of His Kingdom to all of those yet to have a relationship with God. We can do this by proclaiming the gospel by the empowerment of the Holy Spirit.

Let me ask you a question. Do you realize that because you are a Christ follower and Christian faith-filled person, that spiritually you do not belong to this world? That you are a foreigner? The truth of the matter is that you do not fit into this world.

Because you believe that Jesus is the Son of God and that He died for your sins and you turned from your sins, you belong to <u>His</u> world.

For through him we both have access in one
Spirit to the Father. So then you are no
longer strangers and aliens, but you are fellow
citizens with the saints and members of the
household of God. (Eph. 2:18-19)

Then as a brother or sister to Christ, He urges you to steer clear of the things of this world.

Beloved, I urge you as sojourners and exiles to
abstain from the passions of the flesh, which
wage war against your soul. (1 Pet. 2:11)

And to be an ambassador of Christ everywhere you go, you must represent Him in the workplace. Be the Christian example at the grocery store. Represent His Kingdom on social media and be His shining example at every other time.

You will not be perfect all of the time.
Still, He knows that you can be a great
representative when others need it the
most when it is the most important.

You need to know how He wants you to represent Him, so that you understand as an ambassador of Christ how you are to respond at 2 PM on a Thursday when things do not go the way you want them to go. You need to know how He wants you to represent Him, so that you know how to respond when there is someone in need that doesn't look like you or comes from the "bad" side of town. You need to know how He wants you to represent Him, so that you know what to do when someone wrongs you and abuses you.

CHAPTER THREE

Need to Know Info

If you are going to represent the Kingdom of Heaven as an ambassador, then you need to know Jesus wants you to represent His Kingdom. This is one reason why Jesus taught in parables. He was revealing to His people the keys that unlock the mysteries of the Kingdom of Heaven.

What you will see time and time again in these parables is that Jesus used the words "The Kingdom of Heaven is like..." The relevance of this phrase will be explained as we go. What I want you to do is just be aware that the Lord used this phrase more in His parables than in other teachings. It was for a reason, one that will be revealed as we go.

Also, I want to give you some introductory notes on how we are approaching this valuable study, so you understand why I am detailing what I am. I want you to fully understand what a parable is, why the Lord used the characters he did and various other things. This is because this book is meant to explain the riddles not to leave you wondering. That means I will not assume that you know what I am referring to. So, some things may seem elementary to you. But please believe that it is all necessary.

CHAPTER FOUR

What Is A Parable?

Let's begin with defining what a parable is. The word parable is a transliteration of the Greek word "parabole." It comes from two Greek words, "para" (translated "beside") and "ballein" (translated "to throw"). Literally the word parable means "to throw beside," or "to place beside for the purpose of comparing."

We do this all of the time in our daily conversations when we are trying to make a point. We will say – "you know, it's like..." and then we make our point. Jesus did the same thing. He constantly used the word "like" in His parables.

He told them another parable. "The kingdom of heaven is like leaven that a woman took and hid in three measures of flour, till it was all leavened." (Mt. 13:31, 33)

Some have defined the word **parable** as a story by which something real in life is used as a means of representing a moral thought. The narrative of the story is taken from nature or from everyday human experiences. That is why I love the parables. They are real life situations that teach us spiritual truths.

CHAPTER FIVE

Who Are the Characters?

Who then are the characters in Jesus' parables?

God has revealed his truth to us through His interaction with actual people in history. For example, the entire Old Testament revelation is not just God speaking just to "us," but God's interaction with His people, Israel. However, we know that the lessons that are in the Old Testament contain very important *principles* that have application to us today.

The characters in parables do the things we would expect anyone to do in the normal course of events. The characters in parables are not superhuman. They do not perform superhuman feats. They are people just like you and me and your Aunt Sally. Just like us they do what we would expect them to do in the story that Jesus was telling.

For example, a sower going out into a field is going to do what? He is going to sow (plant, scatter) seed. A man finding a great treasure is going to feel how? He's going to feel overjoyed.

The characters are ordinary people. They are meant to be recognizable and familiar. Their actions are to be easily understood because you are meant to see yourself in the stories. After all, truth is found in the most common and ordinary issues of life.

> ***I believe Jesus taught about situations
> and people who were common,
> the kinds of people that we could
> understand. He did this because He
> wanted us to know that spiritual truth is
> not some high and lofty aspiration made
> available to only a select few or to only
> the most spiritual of human beings.***

No, God desires everyone to know the truth. Whether you have a college degree in theology or you barely made it out of the seventh grade, God doesn't want anyone to remain ignorant. Rather, He desires that everyone come to the knowledge of truth because the truth is what sets us free.

> *And you will know the truth, and the truth will
> set you free.* (Jn. 8:32)

Not just that, but the truth (Jesus) frees you from the deception of this world. The truth frees you from the deception within yourself. And the truth frees you from the entrapments of sin and the enemy of your soul.

> ***As the people of God, we must be on a
> relentless quest for the truth
> that is found in Jesus.***

Not Allegories

Let me tell you what a parable is <u>not</u>. A parable is not an allegory. There is a major difference between the two.

An allegory is defined as a figurative application taken from real historical facts or events. An allegory is a literary tool that uses characters, places, and events to represent people and ideas. They are things that have happened and are being referenced. Let me give you an example.

Paul uses an allegory of Abraham's two sons when he was writing his letter to the Galatians.

> *For it is written that Abraham had two sons, one by a slave woman and one by a free woman. But the son of the slave was born according to the flesh, while the son of the free woman was born through promise. Now this may be interpreted allegorically: these women are two covenants. One is from Mount Sinai, bearing children for slavery; she is Hagar.*
> (Gal. 4:22-24)

NOT ALLEGORIES

This is a historical account of real, live people. You can look it up. People knew these people and could corroborate the story historically.

To contrast that, parables speak of supposed events that never really occurred. They are simply stories Jesus used about things that people <u>could</u> understand in order to teach them something that they <u>don't</u> understand. Usually, it starts with something simple and moves to what is profound.

CHAPTER SEVEN

Why the Parables?

The most popular question involving the parables of Jesus Christ is, why did Jesus teach using parables? Even the disciples asked this question.

> *Then the disciples came and said to him, "Why do you speak to them in parables?" And he answered them, "To you it has been given to know the secrets of the kingdom of heaven, but to them it has not been given. For to the one who has, more will be given, and he will have an abundance, but from the one who has not, even what he has will be taken away. This is why I speak to them in parables, because seeing they do not see, and hearing they do not hear, nor do they understand. (Mt. 13:10-13)*

So, the main reason Jesus taught in parables was this:

Reason #1: Jesus taught in parables to <u>conceal</u> the truth from those whose hearts were already rebellious toward God and hardened.

WHY THE PARABLES?

The reason the disciples were blessed to learn is because they had the right attitude towards Jesus and His teaching. But there were those people whose hearts had already been hardened by their own wickedness and rebellion. They were already antagonistic toward God in their thinking. So, it was their heart's attitude that kept them from understanding these parables.

Essentially, Jesus was separating the fakes from the ones who were after the righteous things. He knew how to separate truth-seekers from the curiosity-seekers.

If there is one nugget of knowledge Bible readers know, it is that truth is revealed only to those who want to know the truth. The Lord can see into the heart. He knows a person's true intention.

Jesus was telling these disciples, even if I did speak the truth plainly, these people would not get it. They wouldn't get it because they really don't want to know the truth. Their mouths may say they want the truth, yet their hearts are saying something contrary.

Here is a wise statement for you: you cannot communicate truth to someone who is unwilling to listen.

To those who really want the truth, they will find it when they seek it. Case in point – the disciples of Christ. Those disciples who were genuinely seeking to know the truth would ask Jesus to explain the meaning of the parables. That is when the truth-seekers would be given the answers they sought. Jesus waited until He could speak to only those who were in earnest desire for the meaning.

WHY THE PARABLES?

He did not speak to them without a parable,
but privately to his own disciples he explained
everything. (Mk. 4:34)

Jesus was separating those who were casual observers from those who were committed followers.

"Committed" is the perfect word to use here. It infers that a person has something invested in the game. And aren't that what we followers of Christ should be – invested in this "game" for Christ? Aren't we committed to understanding the Lord, His teachings, and our purpose even searching for the truth in everything? I think so.

You see, that is a problem with too many people today. I believe that we are living in a generation where there's more information readily available but we are in more need of truth than any other generation that has ever lived. The problem is that even though this generation is more <u>needful</u> of truth than any other generation, it is also more <u>resistant</u> to truth than any other generation.

Not Jesus' disciples though. Their hearts and their minds were open and receptive to the truth taught by Jesus.

For to the one who has, more will be given, and
he will have an abundance, but from the one
who has not, even what he has will be taken
away. (Mt. 13:12)

The more receptive you are to the truth, the more truth God will reveal to you. Think about that glorious gift right there. The more available you make yourself for God's glorious truth, the greater stuff He is going to give you. This means when He looks into your spirit and sees your true intention of living for Him, He is going to reveal wisdom, His word, revelation, love, and on and on and on. He is going to reveal His truth.

However, since all of that is true, then it also means the opposite is also true. The more resistant you are to the truth, the more truth God will withhold from you.

This means that it is completely up to you to determine what level of truth God reveals to you. Those people who were not interested in obeying the teachings of Jesus would hear the parables but totally miss the meaning. They would simply brush them off and move on in life.

This is why I speak to them in parables,
because seeing they do not see, and hearing they
do not hear, nor do they understand. (Mt. 13:13)

They have physical eyes but cannot see spiritual truth. They have physical ears but cannot hear spiritual truth. That is why Jesus spoke in parables. To conceal the truth from those who were unwilling to listen and obey.

My prayer for you is that God opens your spiritual eyes so that you can see what is happening in the spiritual world that you are living in.

Jesus spoke about the reasons why certain people missed the meaning of his parables. He said:

For this people's heart has grown dull, and with
their ears they can barely hear, and their eyes
they have closed, lest they should see with their

*eyes and hear with their ears and understand
with their heart and turn, and I would heal
them. (Mt. 13:15)*

What He was saying is that anytime a person is willing to open their eyes and ears to Him, that is when He will heal them. In other words, if someone was not healed it was because they had willingly closed themselves off to His truth. Jesus did not ever promise to heal physically everyone who trusted Him as Savior, but He did promise to heal spiritually everyone who did; that is forgive their sins and bring them into the family of God.

Mark's record of the same account of Jesus' teaching is found in Mark 4:12; his report makes Jesus' meaning very clear:

*To you has been given the secret of the kingdom
of God, but for those outside everything is in
parables, so that they may indeed see but not
perceive, and may indeed hear but not
understand, lest they should turn
and be forgiven.*

Matthew was writing to a Jewish audience, and they would have understood that Jesus was using a figure of speech because of its use in the Old Testament. Mark clarified for a Gentile audience that what Jesus meant was not physical healing, but spiritual healing, that is, being forgiven for sin.

We have to understand here that Jesus is not a cosmic rapist. He is not going to force Himself onto any situation.

WHY THE PARABLES?

Do you remember when Jesus went into the synagogue in Nazareth proclaiming the gospel, and the people were rejecting Him? In fact, the people of Nazareth had already rejected Him previously. Matthew did not say that Jesus was <u>unable</u> to do miracles there, as if His power to do so were shackled by the people's unbelief; Matthew simply stated "οὐκ ἐποίησεν": "he did not do" many miracles there. Jesus' miracles were never just haphazard demonstrations of power. They were always signs pointing to his identity as Israel's Messiah and his being the Son of God. Luke recorded that after Jesus preached in the synagogue:

> *...all in the synagogue were filled with*
> *wrath. And they rose up and drove him out of*
> *the town and brought him to the brow of the hill*
> *on which their town was built, so that they could*
> *throw him down the cliff. But passing through*
> *their midst, he went away. (Luke 4:28-30)*

The crowd was hostile and wanted to kill Him! Why would He have blessed them with His gracious acts of healing? That just doesn't make since to me! Later, in 70 A.D., Jesus would perform a dramatic act of judgment upon the covenant breakers in Jerusalem. He could have performed a miracle of judgment upon the people that day in Nazareth. His decision not to do so was actually an act of mercy on His part.

It was not that the inhabitants of Nazareth had His spiritual power handcuffed by their unwillingness to accept Him; it was because He chose not to work in their behalf because of their rejection of Him and His message.

WHY THE PARABLES?

I have heard false teachers preach that the people's unbelief prevented Jesus from doing miracles. This is a message that unbelievers like to hear, namely that they are more powerful than God and can prevent him from working as he wills. The question that needs to be answered clearly is this: can God override people's unbelief?

My answer is this: the New Testament clearly teaches that all men are sinners who fall short of the glory of God and apart from God's forgiveness, all are doomed to an eternal hell.

Jesus declared in John 8.34 that humans apart from the grace of God are slaves to sin. Can a slave of sin free himself? Absolutely not! The Apostle Paul said in Ephesians 2 that apart from the grace of God people are dead in trespasses and sin.

What Jesus taught, followed by his apostles, was that man <u>cannot</u> save himself. The slave cannot free himself, and the dead man cannot give himself life. It takes the miracle of the new birth, a work accomplished by God and God alone, causing a lost person to be born again. When God does that miraculous act in the life of a sinner, he overrides that person's rejection of God and his unbelief. If God were not able to override the unbelief of a human being, then every person on the planet would be doomed to hell!

Again, the first reason Jesus taught in parables was to <u>conceal</u> the truth from those whose hearts were prejudiced and hardened. Consider that word – prejudiced. It comes from two words: "pre" and "judged." We see that the people in Nazareth had already judged in advance what they were going to believe. So, there was no point in trying to convince them otherwise.

I wonder, are there people who you are dealing with who have closed their eyes and ears to the truth? Have they already made up their minds about what they are going to believe? And if so, do you know what you should and should not do? It's a sad truth that some people just won't listen to nor understand God's truth.

CHAPTER EIGHT

Second Reason

The second reason Jesus taught in parables was to reveal heavenly truth to those whose hearts were open and receptive.

How do you explain something to someone when what you are explaining is foreign to them? You use that which they can relate with to explain it, don't you? That is what Jesus did by using the parables.

Jesus was taking what was known, the earthly truths contained within the parables, and using the known to explain the unknown. He was using the natural to explain the supernatural. He was using the earthly to explain the heavenly. This was done using something they could <u>see</u> and comparing it to something they could not see. Using the material to explain the spiritual. Using the common to explain the uncommon.

It became a wonderful teaching tool. When they understood what Jesus was talking about, they then could gain spiritual insight and make spiritual application to their lives.

SECOND REASON

Now, here is the kicker. It is not enough to simply know about a great thing. You must be able to implement that great thing, idea, ideal, or action. It is not just what you know that makes a difference. It is what you <u>do</u> based on what you know that will change your life.

People claim that knowledge is power. Well, let me tell you that just isn't true. It is part of the right equation, but not the whole thing. Action must be applied first. This means that "applied knowledge" is power. Understanding without application leads you into even greater ignorance because you close the door to any further relationship with God.

Action is required. I have found that the people who seize the most out of life are the ones who take action.

God has given each of us the tools we need to succeed in fulfilling His specific plan for our lives.

So, those who take those tools and passionately act upon that plan are the ones who experience the greatest success. But the ones who ignore those tools, letting them rust away on the shelf, lack achievement.

It is really a simple concept, yet so many still don't get it. So, take a look at your life today. Are you committing yourself to knowledge or are you committing to the application of knowledge? There is a tremendous difference. Applying your God-given knowledge is key to becoming who He means you to be.

CHAPTER NINE

The Third

Let us now move to the third reason why Jesus used parables to teach.

1. To conceal from those who were prejudiced.
2. To reveal to those who were open.
3. **To appeal to their sense of justice.**

Jesus taught in parables <u>to appeal to their sense of justice</u> before they realized that the parable applied to them.

Look at the parable that Nathan told David:

> *The rich man had very many flocks and herds, but the poor man had nothing but one little ewe lamb, which he had bought. And he brought it up, and it grew up with him and with his children. It used to eat of his morsel and drink from his cup and lie in his arms, and it was like a daughter to him. Now there came a traveler to the rich man, and he was unwilling to take one of his own flock or herd to prepare for the guest who had come to him, but he took the poor man's lamb and prepared it for the man who had come to him." Then David's anger*

*was greatly kindled against the man, and he
said to Nathan, "As the LORD lives, the man who
has done this deserves to die, and he shall
restore the lamb fourfold, because he did this
thing, and because he had no pity."
Nathan said to David, "You are the man! Thus
says the LORD, the God of Israel, 'I anointed you
king over Israel, and I delivered you out of the
hand of Saul.'" (2 Sam. 12:2-7)*

The parable appealed to David's sense of justice. The prophet wanted this great man to think of the situation in terms of right and wrong and not who is right or wrong. The parable appealed to David's sense of making things right so that when Nathan revealed that the parable was about him, he would naturally repent and make things right.

Jesus used this approach often when confronting his enemies. One such instance involved the wicked tenants, the classic example found in the book of Matthew.

*"Hear another parable. There was a master of a
house who planted a vineyard and put a fence
around it and dug a winepress in it and built a
tower and leased it to tenants, and went into
another country. When the season for fruit drew
near, he sent his servants to the tenants to get his
fruit. And the tenants took his servants and beat
one, killed another, and stoned another. Again
he sent other servants, more than the first. And
they did the same to them. Finally he sent his
son to them, saying, 'They will respect my
son.' But when the tenants saw the son, they said*

to themselves, 'This is the heir. Come, let us kill him and have his inheritance.' And they took him and threw him out of the vineyard and killed him. When therefore the owner of the vineyard comes, what will he do to those tenants?" They said to him, "He will put those wretches to a miserable death and let out the vineyard to other tenants who will give him the fruits in their seasons."

Jesus said to them, "Have you never read in the Scriptures: "'The stone that the builders rejected has become the cornerstone; this was the Lord's doing, and it is marvelous in our eyes'? Therefore I tell you, the kingdom of God will be taken away from you and given to a people producing its fruits. And the one who falls on this stone will be broken to pieces; and when it falls on anyone, it will crush him." When the chief priests and the Pharisees heard his parables, they perceived that he was speaking about them. And although they were seeking to arrest him, they feared the crowds, because they held him to be a prophet.

(Mt. 21:33-46)

Here Jesus spoke of wicked tenants who refused to pay the owner of the vineyard what he was owed. After sending several emissaries to those corrupt tenants, the owner sent his son, whom the tenants eventually killed out of bitter envy and hatred.

THE THIRD

Obviously, anyone who hears this parable should have a sense of justice growing within them. When the chief priests and Pharisees heard this parable, they perceived that Jesus was really talking about them.

Yet, when Jesus finished telling the parable, look how the Pharisees responded:

> *When the chief priests and the Pharisees heard his parables, they perceived that he was speaking about them.* (Mt. 21:45)

Jesus drew them in emotionally first. Then He hooked them spiritually. He showed them how to agree with the injustice of the situation. He detailed the issue in such a way that it made them crave righteous judgement against the guilty tenants. Then the reality of the situation, the self-comparison set it. That is when they realized that **they** were the real subject of the parable.

The parables are teaching tools. They give good gifts to those who will listen. I encourage you to read each parable. Jesus makes it very clear that to be wise means learning His lessons. We do not have to know everything. But to create the kind of character we are meant to have, absorbing His parables and displaying them in our life is crucial. We must accept His truths then display those truths in our lives.

So, the three reasons Jesus taught in parables was to:

1. Conceal
2. Reveal
3. Appeal

CHAPTER TEN

Don't Overthink It

After learning what a parable is and why the Lord used them, it seems wise to detail how to interpret the parables.

Sometimes Jesus gave the interpretation to the parables, but on other occasions we are left to interpret them ourselves. Due to this fact, I know it means you need to understand a few things in order to properly interpret Jesus' parables.

Interpretation Rule #1: Don't read too much into the parables.

Some make the mistake of reading deep spiritual truths into every minute detail rather than drawing simple truths from the parable. Parables are meant to reveal simple, basic truths to those who are seeking to understand the teachings of Jesus.

Understand that Jesus was speaking to and teaching the general population. This meant that most were uneducated folk. Most did not know how to read, and they were not going to be big on pondering the truths of the universe. They were workers who simply wanted to be told what to do so they could please God and live a good life. Such is why Jesus kept His teachings simple.

Parables are not there to confuse His teaching with endless theological speculation. I am amazed that there are some people who can read almost anything into the Scripture and make it say something that Jesus never intended for it to say. The Lord taught in such a way that He could communicate with people living in that culture. He meant for the simple truths contained in parables to be carried away in the mind of the receiver.

I do not believe that Jesus meant for them to be examined under a theological microscope or dissected to reveal every minute detail. So, when we read these parables, look for the <u>simplest explanation first.</u> Look for the general theme of the parable, then delve deeper into the sub-meanings or sub-themes.

CHAPTER ELEVEN

No New Doctrine

Interpretation Rule #2: You cannot form a new doctrine out of a parable.

You cannot form a new doctrine out of a parable because truth must agree with truth. This is why I say the Bible is its own best commentary and to make sure that you are not trying to make a parable fit what you want. I want you to ask yourself three questions when reading and interpreting Jesus' parables.

Question #1: To whom was Jesus speaking?

In most instances, the intended audience will be His disciples. But on other occasions, the audience will range from publicans and sinners to the scribes and Pharisees. The point in knowing this is that you need to read the Bible with the perspective of the audience to whom Jesus is speaking. Because putting yourself in that audience's shoes steers you towards thinking as that audience would think, act, and respond. To learn the lesson Jesus intended means trying to do all we can to be His audience at that very moment.

Question #2: What did Jesus intend to accomplish by the parable?

This answer may or may not always be obvious. For example, the parables of the mustard seed and the leaven are very brief, but it may offer clear insight into why Jesus taught these parables. When we understand that in some context of Scripture, Jesus had just spoken two parables to His disciples that were somewhat discouraging, the parable of the sower and the parables of the wheat and the tares, He was probably using the mustard seed and leaven to encourage the disciples that while his kingdom would start small, it would eventually encompass all nations; from twelve disciples to the world!

On other occasions, the purpose of the parable will become much more obvious. Some were spoken to those who were more concerned about an outward display of religion than they were the practical application of religion, such as the parable of the Good Samaritan.

Question #3: What is the lesson to be learned?

Every parable has a simple lesson to teach. Some will be more apparent than others. Still, there is a simple lesson to be learned through each parable taught by Jesus. The key to understanding His teachings is to not make the lesson overly complex or highly theoretical. And don't forget that parables were intended to be simple, direct lessons that could easily by remembered, and whose truths would be unforgettable.

Look for the **central** truth in every lesson. Parables contained the "mysteries of the Kingdom of Heaven" (Mt. 13:11) as well as "things which had been kept secret from the foundation of the world" (Mt. 13:35). However, these mysteries and secret things are now revealed in the wonderful gospel of Christ. So, don't overcomplicate things.

CHAPTER TWELVE

For Followers

These parables hide incredible truths for the people of God, revealing how we are to represent the Lord Jesus Christ. Jesus told these parables strictly for His followers. This means that as a Christ follower, these parables are meant for you. This brings me to the next part of the book – the **why.**

What is so great about the parables of Jesus is that there is no doubt He used whatever He saw around Him to instruct. Whatever He and His followers came across – a field of sowers, an unfruitful fig tree, a money lender – He used the life that was happening around Him as an example. He generally referred to something or someone He could see (or the whole group of followers could see) and used it as an example or illustration.

Take for example the sower and the soils. No doubt at the very moment Jesus was telling this parable about the sower, He saw someone sowing seeds. Mostly likely, the whole crowd could see the sower because the Sea of Galilee is ringed with fields, even today. And were you to go there today, you would see sowers sowing seed in the furrows of their fields during this particular time of the year.

Jesus was speaking to them in very common language which they understood because it was their daily activity. It was everyday life for them.

I imagine you would learn much better this way as well. Don't you believe so? Think about which way is better: someone describing a completely foreign phenomenon to you and you trying to picture it without every seeing it, or your being very familiar with something because you see it many times a year.

You are probably going to understand quicker and more surely with the example involving that "thing" you are already familiar with.

The sower and the seed is the first of a series of parables Jesus gave to His disciples. He always started with something they could understand and moved to something they did not understand. He began with something they could see and moved to something they could not see. He started with something natural and moved to something having spiritual significance.

CHAPTER THIRTEEN

Seed and the Sower: The First Type

So, Jesus told a parable.

*And he told them many things in parables,
saying: "A sower went out to sow." (Mt. 13:3)*

The rows would already have been plowed and prepared to receive the seed. The farmer would have a leather pouch loaded with seed hanging over his shoulder. He would reach into the leather pouch and take the seed and broadcast it. This is where the modern word comes from. The farmer actually throwing or broadcasting the seed. He measured out each amount in his hand as carefully as he could so that he could minimize waste. Then he would distribute it as evenly as possible.

Uniformly reaching into the bag and taking the appropriate steps, he broadcast the seed into the furrows. He would go all the way to the end of one furrow, then he would turn and come back down the next, continuing that until he had sown all the seed in the prepared field.

No doubt, Jesus pointed to the farmer that the crowd was watching and made the illustration.

SEED AND THE SOWER: THE FIRST TYPE

And as he sowed, some seeds fell along the path,
and the birds came and devoured them.
(Mt. 13:4)

I want to point out something that is lost in the mix, something that Jesus' followers probably knew but we "modern" non-farming types probably do not. Jesus was more concerned about the soil in this illustration than He was the seed.

This is what I want you to understand.

Focusing on the right thing when learning from God means acquiring the information He urges you to get.

You can read all of the Scripture you want and get little out of it if your focus is not on the right thing.

Again, Jesus was more concerned about the soil than He was the seed. The point of this parable is not the seed; it is the soil. Because without the right soil, the seed can never grow.

You may read this parable and think to yourself, how could seed get on the wayside or the road if the farmer is in the field? Let me expound upon some details.

Obviously, in ancient Palestine, people walked or rode an animal everywhere they went. Many times, they had to travel through the fields. So, fields were basically bordered by beaten paths or roads that were called the "wayside." Remember in the book of Matthew 12 how Jesus and His disciples were walking through the fields and they plucked and ate from it? There were beaten paths around the rows of crops so that the farmers could have access to the entire field. As a result, these beaten paths were uncultivated, and because Israel is very dry, they were also packed hard and dry. They became hard, dry paths, beaten down by the feet of the animals and the people who walked on them.

Seed which fell on these pathways, that fell on this kind of ground, could not penetrate the soil. It would just lie there until the birds would come and eat it. So, the seed was wasted on the wayside.

CHAPTER FOURTEEN

The Second Kind

*Other seeds fell on rocky ground, where they did
not have much soil, and immediately they
sprang up, since they had no depth of
soil, but when the sun rose they were scorched.
And since they had no root, they withered away.*
(Mt. 13:5-6)

Jesus calls the second kind of soil stony or rocky. That does not mean that there were stones in the soil. When a farmer plowed the field, he would plow the stones out of it — unearth them then remove them.

In Palestine, there are large plates of limestone rock that lie beneath the surface and beneath the plow. So, there were times when the farmer could not plow deep enough and wasn't even aware that the layer of stones was there.

So, when seed fell upon those kinds of places, it would burrow down into the ground, but it didn't have much depth of soil. Consequently, it would immediately spring upward. Because what happens is that seed goes down into the soil, it decomposes and that releases its life. In the warmth of the soil and the moisture that is there, it begins to generate. It sends its roots down. But all of a sudden the roots hit the layer of rock and can't go anywhere. So when the sun rises, the plant is scorched because it has no solid root and it immediately withers away.

CHAPTER FIFTEEN

The Third Kind

*Other seeds fell among thorns, and the thorns
grew up and choked them.* (Mt. 13:7)

I remember when I was growing up, my mother had a garden. One of the things that I hated the most was when it was time to weed the garden. Mom said my little hands were perfect for the job.

The key to weeding is to get all of the weeds out. She would always make sure that I didn't just pull the top of the weed off and not get the bottom. Because if I didn't get the root of the weed, what would happen? It would come back stronger than before. And you better believe that weeds can have very strong roots. Because they are just like our struggles in life – the longer we let them fester, the harder they are to get rid of completely.

The seed has to be alone in the soil if it is going to be fruitful and grow.

So, this soil is not weed-free soil. It is deceptive. It has been cultivated, and it looks weed-free, but down in that soil are the seeds or roots of weeds ready to spring up to life. Therefore, when the moisture there coupled with the warmth of the sun, that is when the weed will take growth and grow up fast. Even worse is that a weed will steal the moisture that the seed needs to grow. The weed also takes the nourishment out of the soil also intended for the farmer's seed. This leaves the farmer with a fragile young plant that may not survive.

CHAPTER SIXTEEN

The Best Kind

Of course, that is not the end of the story. Otherwise, it would be pretty senseless to be a farmer.

Other seeds fell on good soil and produced grain, some a hundredfold, some sixty, some thirty. (Mt. 13:8)

This is the good ground. This is ground that is perfect for production. Ground that is deep, soft, rich, and clean of weeds. The reason that Jesus said that the fruit of this soil varies from thirtyfold, sixtyfold, to a hundredfold is because the nutrients in the soil vary from place to place. Some soil may be more acidic than others. It may mitigate against the greatest possible amount of growth. But seed will find its entry. It will find its nourishment and bear fruit. This is the message we believers need to hear, need to understand.

He who has ears, let him hear. (Mt. 13:9)

In other words, Jesus was saying, do you have any idea of what I just said? I am not giving you an agricultural lesson. I am giving you a spiritual lesson. From the natural, obviously they understood. They saw farmers every single day. They understood how farming and sowing seed really worked.

But Jesus wanted them to look beyond the natural and see the spiritual lesson. Understand that He was not talking about natural ears and natural hearing. He was talking about spiritual ears and spiritual hearing.

CHAPTER SEVENTEEN

The Parable Revealed

There is a great truth that Jesus wants you to understand through this parable.

There are only three components involved with this parable: the sower, the seed, and the soil. Now, the parable does not say anything about the sower except that there was one. Jesus just said the sower went out to sow. But we can conclude from later in this chapter who this sower is.

He answered, "The one who sows the good seed is the Son of Man." (Mt. 13:37)

Jesus made obvious what the seed is, too:

When anyone hears the word of the kingdom and does not understand it, the evil one comes and snatches away what has been sown in his heart. This is what was sown along the path.
(Mt. 13:19)

The greatest desire of Jesus is for His people to receive the word of God. He wants us to take that great treasure into our hearts in such a way that it will produce the fruits of the Kingdom of God on this earth. Sound familiar?

THE PARABLE REVEALED

He wants you to be fruitful. He wants you to produce.

> *You did not choose me, but I chose you and*
> *appointed you that you should go and bear fruit*
> *and that your fruit should abide, so*
> *that whatever you ask the Father in my name,*
> *he may give it to you. (Jn. 15:16)*

I believe it breaks the heart of Jesus to see His bride—the church—be spiritually stagnant and unproductive. Hearing this, I pray that you recognize that your mission on earth is to bring forth the fruit of the Kingdom of God so this world can see the Kingdom of God lived out.

The world will never believe what they cannot see. Therefore, for them to believe the Kingdom of God they must see it in our lives. As has already been explained, you are told to be an ambassador for Christ, showing evidence that you are truly experiencing God's Kingdom by displaying righteousness, peace, joy, and a filling of the Holy Spirit.

> *For the kingdom of God is not a matter of eating*
> *and drinking but of righteousness and peace*
> *and joy in the Holy Spirit. (Rom. 14:17)*

The purpose of the parables is so that you can know how to represent the Kingdom of God to this spiritually foreign nation of the worldly system. Right out of the chutes, Jesus taught that the way the world will see the Kingdom of God is to see the fruit of the Kingdom <u>in your life</u>. The only way to bear the fruit of the Kingdom is to allow the word of God to take root in your heart – end of story.

THE PARABLE REVEALED

There is nothing more spiritually productive in your life than learning the word of God, because it is so important to you and to others. This is true because God's people should follow God's revealed purposes and His requirements, which He calls them to do through His word – the Scripture. If you do not do this, and encourage others to do the same, they may either begin to or continue to conform to worldly beliefs, behaviors, and lifestyles.

No matter how perfect or how powerful both the seed and the sower are, it is the soil that makes the difference over whether anything is produced.

The point that Jesus is making here is that you need to get your heart in the right position to receive what Jesus is saying to you. Because if your heart is not right, it makes it so much harder to hear what He has to say.

Alas, here is the thing: if you can't hear what God has to say, it does not minimize or change the messages He is saying. The seed and the sower remain the same. It is only the soil that varies.

Jesus remains the same.

> *Jesus Christ is the same yesterday and today*
> *and forever.* (Heb. 13:8)

The word of God remains the same.

> *The grass withers, the flower fades, but the*
> *word of our God will stand forever.* (Isa. 40:8)

It is the heart that must be prepared to receive the seed.

THE PARABLE REVEALED

The heart is deceitful above all things, and
desperately sick; who can understand it?
(Jer. 17:9)

It is time to get your heart in the place where you can receive the word of God. You say, I attend church, I read the Bible, I hear the word of God. Yet, the physical is not what I am referring to. I am not asking you if you hear the physical word. I am asking if you spiritually hear the word of God.

The Lord was making a very important statement when He stated:

He who has ears, let him hear. (Mt. 13:9)

I'm certain He is speaking to you now through that message.

So, ask yourself, are you hearing what God is saying to you? Because if you are in the church and are a follower of Christ, then His spiritual word is not only supposed to be with you, directing you, it should be <u>in</u> you.

Get your heart right. Get your heart in the spiritual position it needs to be. Because if your heart is not in the right position, you are going to miss out on these messages I'm about to throw at you.

The Hardened Heart

The condition of your heart matters. Don't believe me? Look up the word "heart" in your Biblical concordance. Once you do, you'll see a lengthy listing, showing that God cares about the condition of your heart. And you should too.

I want to discuss first the hardened heart. Now, you may inquire into how a heart can be hardened. You may ask how a heart has anything to do with a sower and some seed. Well, I'm going to tell you.

Look first to the Scripture for answers.

When anyone hears the word of the kingdom and does not understand it, the evil one comes and snatches away what has been sown in his heart. This is what was sown along the path.
(Mt. 13:19)

Remember the wayside was the beaten paths around the rows of crops so that the farmer could have access to all of his field. These paths were uncultivated and not watered. They became hard, beaten paths that were baked by the sun. They were beaten down and trampled on by the feet of the people and the animals who walked on them. Because this ground was unplowed and unprepared, the seed never penetrated it, and the birds could come and quickly snatch the seed before it ever even had a chance to penetrate the ground.

The "seed", as Jesus explained, was the gospel message about how to get into God's kingdom. A person enters the kingdom by placing his trust in the King, Jesus Christ. What Jesus said was that this person "does not understand" the gospel message that was given. He "heard" with his ears the message, but although he heard the good news about salvation and entrance into the kingdom, he does not get it; he does not comprehend the message; he does not grasp it.

The unprepared heart is one that has been trodden down and has become hardened through doubt, fear, and unbelief. The word of God, whether spoken or written, never has penetrated the heart.

> ***Think about this: when God speaks, the enemy will come with doubt and tell lies like, "God didn't really mean that." Or Satan will come with a spirit of fear trying to convince you that you could never be better, achieve that something, or otherwise grow or prosper.***

The enemy has perfected the routine of coming at you trying to attack your faith. Getting you to fail to believe. Trying to convince you that something (whatever that good stuff may be) is not for you. That "good" must be for someone else. Yes, the devil will snatch the word from you through doubt, through fear, and through unbelief. What the enemy has done is to snatch away the seed—it's gone! The evil one may also use such things as false teachers to do this; he may use the fear of man; he may use the individual's own pride to keep him from responding to his need of a savior; but he most often uses the person's love of his own sin.

Now, I have used the terms "enemy," "Satan," and "the devil." But I want to be clear. Those that are aiming to harden your heart are not only those entities found in the spiritual realm. The people and things that are around you on a daily basis can do just as much damage to your heart, soul, and spirit.

You may be one of the unfortunate souls who has allowed life to beat you down. Who has allowed people to walk all over you. They have walked all over you, they have abused you, they have rejected you, they have falsely accused you. Because of that, your heart has become hardened.

It does not take a rocket scientist to understand why orphaned children who spend years being raised by the system rather than loving families are hundreds of times more likely to break the law than the average child. It is because those children are given way too big a dose of the "garbage" that this world can dish out way before they should even know that this earthly world can be... well, just down right horrible at times. Kids raised in state systems deal with tough situations before they should need to. As a result, they grow up tough, with hardened hearts.

The truth of the matter is that far too many people allow the experiences of life to harden their heart from receiving the fresh word of God. You don't have to be raised in an imperfect system to recognize that the world can be rough.

Listen, I don't care what your situation is. There is a greater way to live and it is with God. I don't care how many people have walked all over you. God will never walk out on you. The end all message is: never let the experiences of life become bigger than the word of God to you.

> ***The message of the kingdom was an invitation to be restored to a relationship with the King, Jesus, by repenting of sin and following the will of the King in humble obedience. It's about prospering spiritually by being forgiven of sin and living as a child of God.***

CHAPTER NINETEEN

The Shallow Heart

Another thing that people struggle with is something that may be referred to as a shallow heart. This arises from things you are going through that mess you up so badly that you start to waiver in your belief in God. You fail to believe in what He has said.

*As for what was sown on rocky ground, this is
the one who hears the word and
immediately receives it with joy... (Mt. 13:20)*

Remember, this refers to the large plates of limestone rock that lie beneath the surface there in Palestine. There were times the farmer could not plow deep enough. He wasn't even aware that the layer of stones was there. So, when seed fell upon those kinds of places, it would burrow down into the ground only so far but not deep enough for good growth.

This is the person who gets so excited when they hear the word of God that they are the ones that declare loud and proud – I'm in! They are quick to go out and buy all kinds of Christian workbooks and study guides. They get extremely involved with every church function. They even rush to confess their newfound way of life and try to entice others to join them. They are ready to charge into hell with a water pistol.

However, enthusiasm is not the same as commitment.

I believe we people of God should be enthusiastic and excited about our faith. But my faith does not depend on my level of enthusiasm. The enthusiastic but uncommitted person will never make it through the difficult times in life.

> *...yet he has no root in himself, but endures for a*
> *while, and when tribulation or persecution*
> *arises on account of the word, immediately he*
> *falls away.* (Mt. 13:21)

Enthusiastic but uncommitted people are the shallow soil. When the tough times come (and they will), suddenly the shallow soil people will disappear. They are nowhere to be found. They go right back to who they were before they received the word. They did not realize that there was a cross to bear, and once that they realized that there was a price to pay for following Christ, then they were gone! Tribulation and persecution will manifest unbelievers. They are not really "followers" of Jesus. These kinds of "followers" have no depth.

What is so amazing about these people is how quickly they grow. They come in like a flash of lightning, taking the church by storm. I mean, they are going to win the entire world for Jesus. But they don't realize that there were troubles involved in following Jesus!

Following Jesus is going to cost you something. If you are not willing to pay the price, then you will never have the depth needed to bear solid fruit. Difficulties will come in life. But they come not to destroy you but rather to deepen you.

One of the most difficult things to do in reaching the destiny God has prepared for us is our willingness to be patient in the process.

I know we all want to be superhuman in our faith and get there fast. But it is often the pain in life that leads us towards being great for God. It is that pain of the process that creates real maturity, lasting maturity, and spiritual growth, or deep soil.

So, look, while I believe that excitement is a great characteristic for us to hold, I would rather have some people around me who have depth than have enthusiasm.

CHAPTER TWENTY

The Thorny Heart

*As for what was sown among thorns, this is the
one who hears the word, but the cares of the
world and the deceitfulness of riches choke the
word, and it proves unfruitful.* (Mt. 13:22)

In this case, I believe that the word actually does begin to take root and grow a little. But there comes a moment in their life where their thorns and weeds that also exist in the soil begin to sap all of the nutrients out of the soil. Because the nutrients are gone, the seed is not able to be fed and cannot grow in the way that it needs to grow.

Weeds are indigenous, living naturally in soil. It is the seed that is the foreign element in this equation. After all, have you ever had to go out and plant weeds for them to pop up in the cracks of your sidewalk or in your garden? Of course not, because they grow naturally. The thorns and the weeds were in the soil before the seed was ever planted. This leads me to this statement:

**Your natural heart is more accustomed
to the cares of life than it is to the
word of God.**

The amazing things about weeds and thorns are how resilient and committed to their success they are. They are strong-willed little things, aren't they? Because even though you clear them out before you plant the seed, somehow at least some of them will grow back.

That's the crazy thing about the little things in life. We may not think they are of major concern when they first pop up because we believe they are small matters which are easily rectified. But even small matters can become a major problem or even a lifetime issue is left unchecked. Not to mention that if we do not wipe them out fully the first time that they can keep coming back, hindering us.

In your life you must be careful that the cares of life do not choke out the word of God.

I am not simply talking about sinful things. The cares of life are what Jesus talked about in verse 31 of Matthew 6.

Therefore do not be anxious, saying, 'What shall we eat?' or 'What shall we drink?' or 'What shall we wear?' (Mt. 6:31)

The word of God has promised that you will always have enough. So, when you are worried about how you are going to pay your bills, how you are going to make enough money, how you are going to be able to fix your broken vehicle so you can get to work, recognize that if you are devoted to God that He is devoted to you. He has made you a promise to be there and provide for you.

Do not worry. For those worries and concerns will sap the nutrients of your heart, making it impossible for the word of God to grow within you. Impossible because you are so worried about what this world is asserting rather than what God is promising.

The person who is not willing to give up
money, sex, or his lifestyle for Christ
is not a believer.

God is not "your Father" if you are a person who has abandoned Christ for the world! This is the double-minded man who is not going to receive anything from God, as James said. This person is trying to serve God and money, he has given in to the deceitfulness of riches.

I want to take a small diversion from the main point to fill you in on a little helpful hint. There has been talk about what this life tries to force on you and what God promises.

Yet at the end of the day, you will learn
that all of it boils down to <u>choice</u>.
More specifically, your choice.
You decide the state of your life.

Paul here below was writing as a believer who had learned contentment as part of the sanctification process as a Christian.

Not that I speak in respect of want: for I have
learned, in whatsoever state I am, therewith to
be content. (Phil 4:11, KJV)

You can be happy despite or because of your circumstances. Yes, life is a rapidly changing journey. We never know what to expect around the corner. Still, the one thing we can do is to learn to be content wherever life takes us.

Notice the words Paul uses: "I have learned..." Contentment and yes, even happiness, is not natural. They come to you only when you make up your mind that, no matter where you are, you will choose to be happy knowing that God is there for His children. If a believer walks through the valley, saying, I choose to be happy knowing God is there with me, when I pass through the fire I am happy because God is with me, when I walk through the floods I am happy because God is with me, the believer is choosing to follow God's promises that He will neither leave them nor forsake them. Why? Because they've learned how to be a respecter of His truth. Believing in Him and choosing all the great things that come from Him. So, I appeal to everyone everywhere to make the right choice by choosing Jesus Christ over the "things" of this world.

CHAPTER TWENTY-ONE

Faith vs. Fear

Since I am on the topic of choosing, let me also say that a choice must be made between the faith you have in Jesus and the fear the enemy tries to invoke in you.

Faith and fear cannot coexist in your heart.

They are polar opposites. One is from God; the other is from the devil. Faith will release the power of the word in your heart whereas fear will restrict the power of the word in your heart. Choosing one over the other helps decide what direction your life takes.

Ask yourself what it is that dominates your thoughts. I mean, really take the time to ponder what devours your attention. Do you think mostly about God and His word? Or are you one of the countless people who have settled for the tricks of the enemy and wasted your time and attention on the cares of this life?

I am not trying to shame you or insult you when I say that you may be wasting your life. But if your attention stays on something other than the truth, then it is a wasted effort.

Even more, it is probably a hindering effort because you are not gaining all that you could.

Let me spend half an hour with you and I will be able to tell you what you let have your attention. Am I some great mind-reading genie? Of course not. I'll know what dominates your thoughts by the words that come out of your mouth. I'll know what you put into your body by what comes out of your mouth. If you are always talking about how you fear this or that, then I know you have let carnality overweigh your spirituality. Talking about fear more than faith is a clear sign that you have allowed the cares of this life to choke out the power of the word in your life.

The word "choke" literally means to suffocate. When you think more about the cares of life than you do the word of God, those cares will suffocate the life-giving breath of the word. Which will sap the spiritual life right out of you.

But again, I come back to the word of the moment.

As for what was sown on good soil, this is the one who hears the word and understands it. He indeed bears fruit and yields, in one case a hundredfold, in another sixty, and in another thirty. (Mt. 13:23)

The one who hears the word and understands it and bears fruit does so because the Holy Spirit has done work in his heart; he is a person whom the Father has given to the Son.

Will you choose what the world suggests or will you repent of your sin and trust in Jesus which is what God wants for you? This is the heart that God desires from each of us, a fertile heart. One that is eager to hear and receive the word of God. When the word gets deep inside of them, they begin to bear fruit in their lives. What is that fruit?

Through him then let us continually offer up a sacrifice of praise to God, that is, the fruit of lips that acknowledge his name. (Heb. 13:15) But the fruit of the Spirit is love, joy, peace, patience, kindness, goodness, faithfulness, gentleness, self-control; against such things there is no law. (Gal 5:22-23)

Not everyone will bear fruit at the same level.

As for what was sown on good soil, this is the one who hears the word and understands it. He indeed bears fruit and yields, in one case a hundredfold, in another sixty, and in another thirty. (Mt. 13:23)

The point is – look at your life and evaluate just how much fruit you are bearing.

CHAPTER TWENTY-TWO

The Good Samaritan

Let us switch our attention to another parable so that we can evaluate the lessons of another parable given by Jesus. That parable is the good Samaritan.

In a nutshell, the parable of the good Samaritan found in Luke 10 boils down to the topic of love. More specifically, it is not just what you do that makes the difference in life; it is the love you have for God and the love you have for others that gives you everlasting rewards.

The parable of the good Samaritan is a very familiar parable. The issue with it is that it is seriously misunderstood and misappropriated when it comes to how we are to live this out. Even the world uses the term "good Samaritan" when describing someone who does a good deed or helps someone in need. If you were to have a flat tire on the road and someone stops to help you change the tire, you say, "I had a good Samaritan stop and help me." Or if you send money to an organization that is feeding or clothing people, you might say, "I am a good Samaritan." Obviously, those are things that we should do. But hang on to your seat. That is not what Jesus was teaching through this parable.

Yes, this seems to be a fairly simple parable. It appears to be one that is easily interpreted with a simple point to it, which is: do good to those who are in need and you are a good Samaritan. However, there is a deeper meaning that Jesus had in mind for this teaching, a meaning that lies beneath the surface and speaks to who we really are and should be as the people of Christ.

A Deeper Meaning

Do you remember what I pointed out was the purpose of the parables?

Then the disciples came and said to him, "Why do you speak to them in parables?" And he answered them, "To you it has been given to know the secrets of the kingdom of heaven, but to them it has not been given. For to the one who has, more will be given, and he will have an abundance, but from the one who has not, even what he has will be taken away. This is why I speak to them in parables, because seeing they do not see, and hearing they do not hear, nor do they understand. (Mt. 13:10-13)

Put plainly – to those who really seek the truth, the truth will be revealed. To those who are unwilling to delve deeply into the spiritual matters of life will never truly understand what Jesus is teaching. This is why there are plenty of people confusing what a Christian's role in life should look like.

These are the same people who look at the church, confusing its purpose. They believe that the Bride of Christ is to just do good works like feed the poor and clothe the needy. They use this ideological way of thinking as a means by which to justify social justice. They say that the church is there to help the neighborhood by paying electrical bills or just generally helping those in need. When they cannot, they are somehow missing the point of the good Samaritan way of life. There are many who feel as though the church is here to alleviate poverty and solve all of the social ills that are in society. They would contend that if the church and her members are not focused on such things, that they are not being the people God urges them to be.

> *I want to be clear. Followers of Christ are to help those who are in need as much as they can. Christians are supposed to help others meet their needs in life.*

However, the primary role of the church is not to solve the social injustices of the world. You and your church are not here to alleviate homelessness. You are not simply empowered to end poverty.

The primary role of the church is to make disciples by proclaiming the gospel of the Lord Jesus Christ, teach them to obey Jesus' teaching, and see the power of the Holy Spirit transform the minds of those who come to Christ. By their minds being transformed, their lives will be transformed. They will, as the prodigal son did, "come to themselves." Those individuals who come to Christ were created to be a child of the most high God.

One of the primary roles of s Christ followers is to share the gospel with unbelievers. When people's <u>minds</u> are transformed by the power of the gospel, their <u>lives</u> will be transformed.

If we meet the social needs of people and never meet their spiritual needs, then we are trapped in a <u>works-based</u> religion. Works are not going to earn you eternal salvation, but will earn you rewards in Heaven. Earning is not even the right thought process when living for God. The good Samaritan is not about you earning something. Our salvation is earned by our good deeds. Because the New Testament is very clear as it teaches that salvation is achieved by **<u>faith alone</u>**. *Sola fide*, the Latin phrase for this truth that was used by the reformers, is perfectly summarized in Ephesians 2:8-9:

> *For by grace you have been saved through faith.*
> *And this is not your own doing; it is the gift of*
> *God, not a result of works, so that*
> *no one may boast.*

Those who reject *sola fide* or salvation by faith alone hold to a gospel based on works that differs from the teachings found in Scripture. In Galatians 1:9, Paul condemned such thinking as a false gospel:

> *If anyone is preaching to you a gospel contrary*
> *to the one you received, let him be accursed.*

We either trust and follow Jesus on the path to fan eternity in heaven, or we reject Him and follow a path to eternal punishment. Immortality is ours either way. How it is spent, where it is spent, and with whom we spend it is dependent upon our choices here and now.

CHAPTER TWENTY-THREE

CHAPTER TWENTY-FOUR

Context

Believe it or not, the point of this story is to lead us away from a works-based mentality into a love-based mentality. I say that because of the context in which the story was told.

And behold, a lawyer stood up to put him to the test, saying, "Teacher, what shall I do to inherit eternal life?" (Lk. 10:25)

Let's be frank, this man wasn't interested in the truth. He was only interested in trapping the Lord and putting Him in a corner. All of the details involved with this example illustrate this truth. Let's look at some facts.

The fact that the lawyer "stood up" means that he was trying to intimidate Jesus with this question. He stood in His face to ask a question that he should have known the answer to because, by being a lawyer, he would have been an expert in the Scriptures.

He wasn't a criminal lawyer. He wasn't a civil lawyer. He was a lawyer of the Old Testament Law. He was part of the religious establishment. He was there to make Jesus look bad. That was why, when he asked the question, look how Jesus responded:

> *He said to him, "What is written in the Law?*
> *How do you read it?" (Lk. 10:26)*

In other words, you should know the answer to your own question because you are an expert in the Old Testament Law.

> **People usually know the answer to the**
> **question of what is right and wrong.**
> **They are just unwilling to confront the**
> **fact that they are not living by what they**
> **know is right.**

God has given us the written word of God and the witness of the Holy Spirit to show us what is right and what is wrong. We just need the fortitude to step up and acknowledge that we are not doing what is right.

So, look how the attorney responded to Jesus' question. He references two Old Testament Scriptures to give his answer:

> *And he answered, "You shall love the Lord your*
> *God with all your heart and with all your soul*
> *and with all your strength and with all your*
> *mind, and your neighbor as yourself."*
> *(Lk. 10:27)*

He was pulling from Deuteronomy 6:4-5 and Leviticus 19:18, which are two familiar Scriptures that sum up the entire law of God.

CONTEXT

*On these two commandments depend all the
Law and the Prophets.* (Mt. 22:40)

This lawyer answered correctly. He said exactly what
he needed to say, and he answered exactly as he should have
answered, which was confirmed by Jesus.

*And he said to him, "You have answered
correctly; do this, and you will live."* (Lk. 10:28)

But although the lawyer knew the law, he was not
living it. Jesus was showing him his failure to be obedient to
the whole Law. The Israelites were to encourage strangers to
settle among them so that they might be brought to the
knowledge and worship of the true God. With this in view,
they were commanded to treat them not as aliens, but as
friends, on the ground that they themselves, who were
strangers in Egypt, were at first kindly and hospitably
received in that country.

Jesus told the parable to bring conviction to the heart
of the lawyer. It is only when a man realizes that he has
broken the moral law of God that he is moved to seek God's
forgiveness. Rather than affirming the lawyer's faithful
obedience to God's Law, Jesus was pointing out his utter
failure to do so. We must not only know the word of God; we
must live it every day.

CHAPTER TWENTY-FIVE

For Love

I'm unhappy in saying that there are too many people in the church doing the right thing but doing it for the wrong reasons. They are religious but they are not righteous. They are good but they are not godly. They pretend to be pious but they are not pure.

This parable is not just about doing good to others. It is about the motivation behind doing good to others. Never get caught up in doing good things just because you are supposed to. It is not what you do that matters the most. It is why you do it.

There will be those who stand before God whose soul is saved. Still, their works will be burned up. Not because they were the wrong things to do but rather because they were done with the wrong motivation.

If we do anything out of obligation rather than love for God and others, we have lost our reward.

Could that be why Paul said in 1 Corinthians 13:3:

*If I give away all I have, and if I deliver up my
body to be burned, but have not love,
I gain nothing.*

Examine your heart and make certain that what you do comes out of an intense and powerful love for God and for people. Any other reason will cause what you do to be lost in the fire and mean nothing.

So again, this parable is not only about doing good to others, it is about the motivation behind those actions that truly matters.

Luke 10:29 is where we gain an understanding of the mindset of how the lawyer felt about things and what his intent was.

But he, <u>desiring to justify himself</u>, said to Jesus, "And who is my neighbor?" (Lk. 10:29)

If you are walking in truth, you never have to justify yourself. The truth is its own best defense. If you always tell the truth, you never have to try to remember what you said and who you said it to. Truth never has to justify itself.

This man (lawyer) was so bound by religion that he was oblivious to the fact that he was not right with God. He was oblivious to the fact that he was not righteous simply because he was so religious. He may have been doing many of the right things. Still, he did not have eternal life.

My desire is to help you get away from a "religious" mindset that focuses on outward performance and get you to a position where you get away from the way things have always been done and replacing them with righteous actions for the right reasons.

I want to help you break free from the mindset of "it's what I do that makes me righteous." Because it's not just what you do or how you act. It is doing the right things for God with the right motivation.

Living in this world, being filled with fleshly feelings and physical desires convinces us that things, thoughts, and actions are the path to everything, and that through them is how we obtain happiness, so it must be how we obtain holiness.

> **It is not only what we do that matters.
> It is the <u>why</u> behind it all that truly
> makes the difference.**

It's our character, people! Character is what matters, the moral and ethical values that form who we are. This means helping others out of love, being the best version of ourselves, trying to imitate our Lord.

> **If our motivations are right, then we will
> never lack the conviction to do the right
> thing in the sight of God.**

If this lawyer was loving his neighbor according to the Law, then why didn't he have eternal life? Because the Law taught that not everyone was your neighbor. Because Jesus revealed what the Law taught about your neighbor.

> *You have heard that it was said, 'You shall
> love your neighbor and hate your enemy.' (Mt.
> 5:43)*

Clearly, this man didn't believe that his enemies were his neighbors. He believed that his neighbor was the person who looked like him, believed like him, worshipped like him, and lived like him. The religious leaders in first-century Palestine did not love their neighbors. They did not love strangers. Furthermore, they didn't even love other Jews. All they loved were the people who were part of their very narrow, elite group. They had their own definition of who their neighbor was, and they were content with that.

Ask yourself if you think it is easy to love the person who believes exactly as you do. Who looks just like you do? Who acts just like you do? Who lives the same lifestyle you do?

But what about the person who doesn't look like you? What about the person whose views are contrary to yours? The person who does not believe as you do? What about the person who not only has a different religious view but also a different lifestyle? Or is of a different color? Can you say that you truly love them despite the huge differences?

***The fact remains that it requires much
more to love that person than it does the
person who agrees with you and sees
things the same way as you see them.
The reason is because it's not very easy.***

CHAPTER TWENTY-SIX

Righteousness' Sake

Some will make the claim that they love others because of their religion. At first glance, some Christians would lean towards agreeing with this stance. But I want to help others gain the understanding of God in this subject.

Let me start off by pointing out what the Lord had to say about loving others:

For if you love those who love you, what reward do you have? Do not even the tax collectors do the same? And if you greet only your brothers, what more are you doing than others? Do not even the Gentiles do the same?
(Mt. 5:46-47)

Religious people will love other people based on how <u>they</u> see them. Righteous people will love other people based on how God sees them.

What about the person who doesn't have the same skin color as you do? What about the person who comes from a different cultural background than you do? What about the person who has a different political opinion than you do? Are you willing to love that person in the same way you love the person who is just like you?

Let me take that one step further. Are you willing to love that person in the same way you love yourself? Do you want that person to reach their God-given potential just like you do the person you agree with?

The parable is not about the amount of _good_ you do for others. It is about the amount of _love_ you have for others.

It is easy for us to look at people and judge them based on the commandments. For example, we might shun them because they have committed adultery. Or we might judge them because we discovered that they cheat or lie.

The fact is that we are not supposed to be shunning sinners. We, as faithful followers of Christ, must be attracting others, bringing them in towards us so that they will be attracted to the Lord.

Let me ask you this: do sinners want to be around you? That seems like a loaded question because the Spirit within us is diametrically opposite of the spirit that is in the world. Because of that, we think that the people of the world will be opposed and won't spend any time with us. But stop for a moment and look at this verse found in the book of Matthew:

> *And as Jesus reclined at table in the house,*
> *behold, many tax collectors and sinners came*
> *and were reclining with Jesus and his*
> *disciples. (Mt. 9:10)*

Jesus was in Matthew's house for dinner and the publicans and sinners did not say, "Oh, there's that new teacher... let's go have dinner somewhere else!" They wanted to be close to Him to see what He was all about. There was something attractive about Jesus, and they were not afraid of being condemned or criticized; otherwise, they would not have hung around.

> *I have to think it was because Jesus was filled with so much compassion and mercy for these people that they were drawn to that compassion and mercy. They knew He was one they could come to just as they were and receive the help they needed.*

I just wonder, do the people of the world think that way about us believers in Christ? Can they come into a church and expect to feel compassion and mercy, or do they stay away because they know they will be criticized and condemned?

Are people attracted to you because they know they will find help for their problems from you? Or do they avoid you because they know they will only receive religious platitudes? Think about that for a moment. Think about how we should act to attract others towards us. Ask yourself what you are doing to draw others in. Are you displaying those same qualities that Jesus displayed? Are you attracting others towards you?

> *Moving on, I want to explain to you that people will never change what they do until they are willing to change who they are. So, stop trying to change what*

people do and start working with
who they are.

CHAPTER TWENTY-SEVEN

Back to the Parable

Let's get back to our parable of the good Samaritan.

Jesus replied, "A man was going down from Jerusalem to Jericho, and he fell among robbers, who stripped him and beat him and departed, leaving him half dead." (Lk. 10:30)

Jerusalem is 3,000 feet above sea level and Jericho is 1,000 feet below sea level. The road between Jerusalem and Jericho is only seventeen miles. So, you are going down a very steep decline. It is a windy road filled with dramatic drops and rocks providing ideal hideouts for robbers. It is a scary place.

History notes that for centuries after the New Testament period, this was a highway that literally featured robbers and bandits.

A favorite site of Arab robbers was the Pass of Adummim. Adummim is a form of the Hebrew word "blood," "blood pass." This was a place of death, a place of significant bloodshed.

The man in our story was not just robbed. He was stripped, beaten, and left half dead. He was left probably with just his undergarments and that's it. Every possession he had in his sack that he must've been carrying, as they did on a journey, even his clothes that he was wearing, they took.

This man was in a desperate situation, one in which he was not able to help himself.

This is exactly where many people are right now. They are in a situation where they cannot help themselves. There is nothing they can do. And the worst part for them is that some of the people who are in a position to help are saying they got themselves into this mess, let them get themselves out of it. And that may be true; maybe the choices they made did get them where they are, but they are in a position where literally there is nothing they can do to get themselves out. Without assistance, they will spiritually and emotionally die on the roadside. They have been beaten by the enemy. They have been stripped of their dignity Stripped of their self-respect. The enemy has left them for dead.

The question that remains is, how will you respond?

*Now by chance a priest was going down that
road, and when he saw him he passed by on
the other side. (Lk. 10:31)*

The lawyer listening to the story might have been filled with a little hope. After all, a priest was somebody who, like the lawyer, knew the Old Testament, knew you were to show kindness, knew you were to minister to strangers. But the priest passed on the other side.

Jesus used very strong language by using the Greek term **anti**. It means he went against. That means that he went on the opposite side of the road. The priests moved as far as he could await from where the injured man lay, totally ignoring this man, showing complete indifference. He shunned him, and he was lying there in critical condition.

The priest represents religious entitlement. This priest was from the tribe of Aaron, which meant by birth he was entitled to the priesthood. His position was granted to him by birth, so he had no way of identifying with this beaten man whatsoever. His **position** stood in the way of loving this man.

> *There are some people who have been in a clerical position for so long that they are oblivious to the needs around them.*

Learn from these people. Do not become so spiritually high and lofty that you miss the needs of people around you. You should never let your position become a detriment to your love for other people. Recognize that at the foot of the cross, we are all sinners in need of the grace of God.

> *Our God is more concerned about righteousness than He is about pouring out His judgment, a truth that is evidenced by so many great lessons in the Bible.*

Sodom and Gomorrah were wicked, this we all know. But we many times forget the conversation that Abraham had with God before the fire and brimstone destroyed the city. God was simply looking for someone righteous in that city. He was more concerned about finding righteousness than He was pouring out judgment. But because of a lack of righteousness, God had no choice but to pour out judgment.

In His grace, He rescued Lot and his family out of that city before judgment came. As I read this passage, I was reminded of how God doesn't want to judge people. In fact, He is looking for righteousness, so He doesn't have to judge. That is why He poured out his judgement on Jesus, so He doesn't have to judge us! When you accept and fully believe the finished work of Christ at Calvary, you escape the judgment of God.

There is no reason to be like Lot's wife, who looked back at God's judgment.

The judgment for sin is behind you at Calvary. If this is true for you, then it is and can be the same for others.

Let us get back to the New Testament example, back to the parable.

> *So likewise a Levite, when he came to the place*
> *and saw him, passed by on the other side.*
> (Lk. 10:32)

He was from the tribe of Levi, son of Jacob, but not the family of Aaron. This meant the man was not from a priestly family, but he still assisted in the temple. Levites worked on the liturgy. They took care of the facilities. They prepared the sacrifices. They did the work that priests didn't do in the temple.

The Levite represents religious engagement.

This man was thinking of all the wrong things. He told himself that he was just too busy to stop and help. He worried himself with maintaining his duties instead of displaying the character he was supposed to be exhibiting each and every day. He worried about tradition rather than application.

He is not alone. Many of us are too busy "doing the work of the Lord" to actually do the work of the Lord.

Look, I'm not telling you not to study the word or stay out of your Bible. I want you to work hard in your study of the word. But may the hard work you do not blind you to the legitimate needs of those around you.

Two Men

*But a Samaritan, as he journeyed, came to
where he was, and when he saw him, he had
compassion. (Lk. 10:33)*

Jesus indicted the religious establishment and introduced a hated man. The fact the Samaritans even existed made them evil in the sight of the Jews. They were a blight on the world. They had been regarded as evil all the way back to the time of Jeroboam. They were considered evil because they intermarried with the Gentiles when the Northern Kingdom was occupied. They were considered evil because they tried to disrupt the rebuilding of the Jewish city and the temple when they came back from the captivity. They were considered half-breed traitors. They were called Samaritans as a derogatory term.

Think about what is being explained here in this parable. Two men represented the Jewish establishment, two men who thought that they loved God and loved others as themselves, had absolutely no love. In other words, their supposed dedication to God was bankrupt.

These two men were religious yet failed to meet the basic principles of the law. They did not love their neighbor.

They did not love strangers. They didn't love their enemies. But this Samaritan, who was an outcast, demonstrated the quality of loving your neighbor as yourself.

He went to him and bound up his wounds,
pouring on oil and wine. Then he set him on his
own animal and brought him to an inn and
took care of him. (Lk. 10:34)

The Samaritan must have knelt down, analyzed, evaluated, assessed, diagnosed his condition and his needs, and gave careful attention to the entire situation. Then, after considering the situation, he took action.

This man bandaged up the assaulted man's wounds. The Samaritan man most likely used part of the clothing he was wearing as rags to first clean this man's wounds then dress them so as to help stop the bleeding. Then, he probably took the oil and wine which people always traveled with for preparation of their meals and poured them on the battered man. His was an act of true love.

It needs to be explained that the word for **poured** is one inferring heavy use, meaning a kind of lavish pouring.

Then, since the man could not walk because of his terrible wounds, the good Samaritan picked him up and put him atop his own animal as he surely walked all the way to the inn where he paid someone to stand in care for him.

Perspective

...brought him to an inn and took care of him.
(Lk. 10:34b)

The Greek word for "inn" is **pandocheion**. **Pan** means "all." So, this is a place was an inn for all – an inn for everyone.

This is not like you would think of the Holiday Inn or any other kind of inn that you would stay in. This was a rough, tough roadside lodging. It was the kind of place that would be used out of necessity, not luxury. You would only want to be there if it were an emergency that got you in from some danger or because you just couldn't go any further.

Then, as if the things the good Samaritan were not enough, the next day when the love-filled man was ready to continue his trip, he took out two denarii and gave them to the innkeeper. That was a day's wage back then.

Just to let you know how much you had to pay for an inn, not too long after this there is some literature that has indicated that a board was found, some kind of sign board from an inn in a city in the Roman Empire. The nightly rate cost one thirty-second of a denarius. One thirty-second of a denarius would mean that the man could have stayed at the inn for two months!

Here is the point I want you to get. This man not only took care of the struggling man's needs, he also made sure the man would be taken care of until he was healthy enough to be on his own.

> ***Love is more than giving money to poor people. It is more than just giving food to hungry people. Love is putting people in a position where they are able to be healed and live beyond just the moment.***

We try to make love a tricky topic, but it should not be.

> *In this is love, not that we have loved God but that he loved us and sent his Son to be the propitiation for our sins.* (1 Jn. 4:10)

Ask yourself, have you trusted the definition of love by choosing to do another person good? Maybe you simply have not taken enough time to study what the Lord has to say about the matter. Or maybe you have closed your ears to the issue.

I remember when I was young, hearing all the scathing messages that chastised the congregation about being lukewarm in our love for God and how that lack of love was leading us to compromise. I remember feeling guilty for somehow not doing enough to show God how much I loved Him. I became confused about what God was requiring of me, and it led me through some spiritually troubling times. Then I read the verse again. Love is not defined by how much we love God but rather by how much God loves us. It can become discouraging when our focus is only on what we do for God rather than what God has done for us. It is when we focus on the incredible love our heavenly Father has shown us in sending Jesus to be our propitiation that we are inspired and motivated to do more for Him.

> ***Today I challenge you to take the focus off of what you are doing for God and invest the time thinking about how much He has done for you.***

The picture of love is not our great religious works but rather the Son of God doing the work for us at Calvary. Remember that.

Love is a lifestyle of helping people with more than just a handout. Love is empowering them to live a life beyond the moment they have been robbed and stripped naked by the enemy. Put as plainly as I can put it: love is not just an act, it is a lifestyle.

Look how Jesus completely grabbed his audience's attention with a question. Look again at the way the lawyer framed his question:

> *But he, desiring to justify himself, said to Jesus, "And who is my neighbor?"* (Lk. 10:29)

The lawyer was asking Jesus who it was he was supposed to love. But Jesus challenged him with another question:

Which of these three, do you think, proved to be a neighbor to the man who fell among the robbers? (Lk. 10:36)

He was saying, this is not about who your neighbor is and whom you are to love. This is about whether you are that neighbor who loves at all times. This is not about who is qualified to be loved. This is about being that neighbor who loves in an unqualified way.

Forget trying to qualify who deserves your love. Just demonstrate love which knows no qualification.

If you think about all of your own shortcomings, then you will know that none of us <u>deserves</u> to be loved unconditionally. All of us are sinners falling short of the mark. Yet, Jesus loves us anyway, and He knows we do not meet the mark, that we do not measure up. Still, He loves us anyways. That is the kind of character we need to display toward others in life.

This story is not a dissertation on how you should treat people. It is too simple to say this is a story about going to the other side of the road and hugging someone who is down on their luck, broke, homeless, or whatever other slight is involved in their life. This is about salvation. This is about eternal life. This is about loving God perfectly, which none of us have the ability to do.

We need the mercy and grace of God to give us the desire to love people in the way that only He can love them.

It helps to see yourself in the right way. Your self-portrait will help determine the response you have to this world.

In verse 28, Jesus told the lawyer,

"You have answered correctly; do this and you will live." Jesus challenged him, "If you want eternal life, fulfill the law. Do this and live."

Now, if you know your Bible, you should be asking, "Why in the world was Jesus telling him to do that? That is not the gospel message! Why didn't Jesus tell the man, 'Place your trust in me; believe in me'?"

The reason was that there was an important issue that Jesus wanted the lawyer to consider, and that was how the man viewed himself.

The gospel message does not mean anything to a person if that person thinks that his relationship with God is just fine. They compare themselves to other people who sin much graver sins than they do, and so, by comparison, they look pretty good.

This was exactly the case with the lawyer. His question to Jesus revealed that he was in this very mode of justifying himself before God, "And who is my neighbor?" He was self-righteous and thought that perhaps Jesus had a little different definition of who a neighbor is; other than that, he was quite sure that God was very happy with him. He was not aware of his true condition before a holy God. He was already sure that he was in a good relationship with God because he was convinced that he was already a righteous man. However, the Old Testament declared in Leviticus 19:34:

You shall treat the stranger who sojourns with
you as the native among you, and you shall love
him as yourself, for you were strangers in the
land of Egypt: I am the Lord your God.

That statement was in Torah, in the Law of Moses; Jesus knew that the lawyer had not done that. Men like the lawyer to whom Jesus was speaking only loved the traditionalists in their little group. They did not even love other Jews who did not meet their standards of religion. His question was nothing more than a justifying of himself, as he challenged Jesus in a mocking tone, "Maybe you'd better tell me who my neighbor is."

Jesus' story was about pointing out the lawyer's utter failure in the sight of God to do one of the most basic truths that the Law taught: to love your neighbor.

All of the Law and the Prophets hung on two truths: love for God and love for neighbor. His failure to love his neighbor meant that he was desperately in need of God's forgiveness. He needed to be born again, but he was totally oblivious to his own need.

I have always wondered why some people are so negative and pessimistic about life; why they are so quick to give up on others. I am puzzled by those who have no problem finding out what is wrong in every situation and with everyone around them.

The answer that I have come up with is that these people have a negative self-portrait, and it has tainted how they look at the world around them. That is a sad reality for too many people.

How you look at yourself is how you look at life.

If the perspective you have of yourself is right, the perspective you have on the world around you will be right. So, I encourage you to listen to how you talk about yourself. Love yourself as well. Consider what words you use. If your language is full of negative self-talk and your mind is full of pessimistic thinking, ask God to change that within you. Look at the lessons like this parable and develop the king of love it takes to not only love yourself but also love others.

Jesus didn't tell this story to make you feel guilty about not giving your money to poor people. It's not to make people feel guilty about not taking care of those that are suffering. This story is designed to make us realize we cannot love God perfectly without the mercy of Jesus. We cannot love others perfectly without the mercy of Jesus. We can't even love ourselves without the mercy of Jesus. We must run to the One who alone can provide the strength we need to love, period.

CHAPTER THIRTY

Persistent

I want to try to move towards a truth. That truth? Only that if you are going to succeed spiritually in these last days, you are going to have to be persistent. Now let me go forth tying these two topics (God's parables and persistence) together.

I urge you to recognize how we, as the ambassadors of Christ and Kingdom to this world, are to properly represent His Kingdom.

To do that I am going to utilize the lesson of a somewhat strange story. It is strange because of how some interpret this story. Some equate it with somehow Jesus comparing our heavenly Father to the unjust judge, which of course is not the case.

This parable is a story of contrasts, not comparisons. Here we see in the book of Luke an example of a persistent widow that demonstrates that God is not like the judge and we are not like the widow. We see this truth because we know our Father and understand that He doesn't need to be nagged or manipulated into acting on our behalf. His care for us is not generated by our wearing him out with requests.

No one likes to be around nagging people. We all know what I'm talking about. We have been at the store with that parent stuck with that overly negative child or children who go on and on and on about getting whatever they want, so much so that the parent finally gives in and gives the child or children what they want. That is not how God works.

Believers of Christ are unlike the helpless widow in the sense that this widow did not know or have any relationship to the judge, whereas we are the children of God. This woman had no advocate, whereas we have Jesus as our advocate, and that's a huge difference. Let me get into why this is true.

CHAPTER THIRTY-ONE

Jesus' Audience

Luke 18:1 gives us the key to the interpretation of the parable, "And he told them a parable to the effect that they ought always to pray and not lose heart." To whom was Jesus referring when he said, "he told *them*"? To whom was Jesus referring when he said, "that *they* ought always to pray and not lose heart"? Who are "they"?

You know that the chapter divisions were not created by Luke. If you were reading this in context, you would know that Jesus was addressing his disciples. Luke 17:22 gives us the context of the individuals who were being spoken to:

And he said to the disciples, "The days are coming when you will desire to see one of the days of the Son of Man, and you will not see it."

Jesus was not addressing twenty-first century Christians about the problems in their daily lives! He is speaking to the Twelve, telling them about the judgment that was coming on the covenant breakers in Israel.

The parable was an encouragement to His disciples not to give up praying as they awaited for the fulfillment of his prophecy, which came true exactly as Jesus said it would in 70 AD when the Roman army destroyed the city and the temple. Every stone was torn down exactly as Jesus said that it would happen: "there will not be left here one stone upon another that will not be thrown down" (Matthew 24:2).

The context is clear about the meaning of the parable, and it was not about the little problems in our lives in the twenty-first century, but the catastrophic events that were impending upon Jerusalem as prophesied by our Lord. Before judgment fell in 70 AD, Jesus told his disciples that they would suffer greatly. They were not to lose heart, but to pray for God's purposes to be carried out in His time.

***We must always be persistent in prayer
while enduring persecution awaiting
coming judgment.***

CHAPTER THIRTY-TWO

Seeking Justice

There are two main subjects involved with this lesson: the widow and the judge, with each character being on the opposite end of the spectrum.

You have a woman and a man. The man is in a position of power while the woman is powerless. The man is prosperous, the woman penniless. The judge was in an exalted position with great authority and the widow was in a humble position without anyone to protect her while she was legally vulnerable and exposed.

If you understand Biblical culture, it was very uncommon for a woman to be able to own property or have any say in legal matters. So being a widow, even something as simple as retaining her husband's possessions as an inheritance could be legally complicated. Many widows were taken advantage of. They were ripped off and no justice was served to them by the legal system.

Jesus, when telling the story, does not detail exactly what had happened to this woman because that was not the point of the parable.

We do know that some criminal activity had been committed against her because she was crying out for justice for the crime that had been committed against her. She may have been beaten. She may have been robbed. Or, if she was abused or taken advantage of, she obviously wanted justice for what had happened to her and she knew exactly who had done it to her because of what is said in Scripture:

Give me justice against my adversary.
(Lk. 18:3b)

This widow was not content to simply sit back and do nothing to pursue justice against her adversary. She was not going to sit idly by and accept the fact that she had been robbed, abused, or taken advantage of. She was not going to let it drop until justice was served and she was restored whatever had been taken from her.

As the ambassadors of the Kingdom of God, we cannot just sit back and allow our adversary to take what is rightfully ours and act like there is nothing we can do about it.

There has to come a time that as a child of the Most High God, you cannot just sit back and allow your adversary to take what is rightfully yours and act like there is nothing you can do about it. There has to come a time that as a child of God, you do something about what the adversary is trying to do against you. I mean, it's not like you don't know what the enemy's objective is.

The thief comes only to steal and kill and destroy. I came that they may have life and have it abundantly. (Jn. 10:10)

But too many times we sit around and act like there is nothing we can do about it. Too many believers are accepting life. Accepting defeat. Accepting what the enemy brings against them as if they have no choice in the matter. This is the hand I have been dealt so I just need to accept it. We complain to each other how much the devil is attacking us and everything that is seemingly going wrong, failing to realize that we don't have to accept what happens to us as if there is nothing we can do about it.

You are not helpless nor are you hopeless. You are a child of the Almighty God.

You have the power of heaven living within you through the Holy Spirit. So why would you accept life as if there is nothing you can do about it?

You need to get up like this widow and realize that you don't have to take the fact that the enemy has spiritually assaulted you, molested you, stolen from you. Instead, you need to take on the mentality of this woman.

This little woman was not content to allow her adversary to get by with what he had done to her. So, what could she do about it? Actually, there were three ways to pursue justice in Biblical culture.

First of all, you might pay off the judge. The issue with this salutation is that the woman had no money.

Secondly, you might threaten the judge. The problem is that the woman is a poor and weak widow who doesn't have the physical strength to threaten this man.

Thirdly, you would persist. You would have to muster up the courage to just keep marching forward in the face of adversity for the sake of justice.

I bring this to you because in the spiritual sense, that is exactly where we are when we have been molested and robbed by the adversary. Our situation may be one where we can't physically find justice through money or any other carnal means. This is a spiritual battle, not a carnal one.

*For the weapons of our warfare are not of the
flesh but have divine power to destroy
strongholds. (2 Cor. 10:4)*

Just like this woman couldn't pay off the judge to get justice, you can't use some earthly or fleshly means to receive the justice you are looking for.

Focusing too much on the flesh while silencing the lessons for the spirit creates problems, not solutions.

Here is the thing. If we would pray about our battles as much as we talk about our battles, the victory would come so much sooner.

CHAPTER THIRTY-THREE

Intimidator

You can't intimidate or threaten the devil. You can't get up and holler and scream and jump up and down and expect your adversary to run from you. Believe me, the devil is not scared of you. He has been manhandling people for millennia. But what he is afraid of is the Jesus who lives within you.

Then he said to me, "This is the word of the LORD to Zerubbabel: Not by might, nor by power, but by my Spirit, says the LORD of hosts."
(Zech. 4:6)

As a servant of God, this message is meant for you. Nothing we do can compare to God's work done through you. Not military might, political power, nor human strength can accomplish His purpose if we are not enabled by the Holy Spirit. Only as the Spirit continues to guide and empower your life will you accomplish God's plans for you. This is precisely why Jesus continues to baptize his followers in the Holy Spirit and why you must be persistent in refusing to be intimidated by your adversary.

Just like this widow, you cannot give up until you know you have overcome what the adversary is trying to do to you. But you cannot give up. You're giving up too easily. You are throwing in the towel too quickly. You are hanging up the gloves before the fight is over.

If there is anything that I want you to take out of this parable it is that you cannot quit until you know you have the victory.

You can't quit until you know you are justified from what the enemy has brought against you. You can't quit until you know you have overcome. Because that is who you are. You are an overcomer. You are not a loser. You are not a has-been. You are a child of the Most High God. Knowing hat, ask yourself these questions:

Why are you just sitting there letting the adversary get away with what he is trying to do against you and your family?

Why are you letting the enemy attempt to divide and destroy your marriage, or anything else?

And if you are, then it is time for you to learn a great lesson from this little widow.

CHAPTER THIRTY-FOUR

Persistence

I want you to learn a little something from this widow. That lesson being: <u>you need to persist until you win.</u>

But look what she is up against:

He said, "In a certain city there was a judge who neither feared God nor respected man."
(Lk. 18:2)

If the man does not fear God that means he doesn't care about doing the right thing. He does not care about justice. He does not care about righteousness. Point blank explanation is that he doesn't care about anything good. He is a selfish myopic god unto himself who does not care about the word of God or the Law of God. to him, there are no consequences for right and wrong, no heaven and no hell. He is a law unto himself.

On top of that, he doesn't love people. Clearly this woman means absolutely nothing to him. She is like a piece of trash that is lying beside the road. He is not concerned about her. Nothing about her tugs on his heart strings. She means nothing to him. But that does not stop her from persisting in her request to be avenged from what her enemy has done to her. She pursued him persistently.

Think about how that scenario would have gone. As he strolls to work in the morning, there she is trying to get a moment of his time. She was saying, I have this issue. He probably moves on, saying he is too busy to help her right now.

"Good morning, Judge. I know your time is precious, but please let me just walk with you to fill you in on what is happening. Could you please take a moment to ponder my case?"

Then, out he comes for a lunch break. She is there once more. "Again, I know how busy you still are. I don't want to bother you. It's just that if you take one minute to hear the details..."

On the way home, you guessed it, there she is. "Hey, Judge. Good to see you again." And she is talking to him about the case in front of family, friends, coworkers, and colleagues.

In other words, even though she knows she is dealing with an evil man, she doesn't give up until she gets what she knows is rightfully hers. And eventually, like a cage-fighting granny who gets the judge in a clinch, he has finally had enough. "Okay, I give in. I relent," he cries. And he gives her the justice which she is demanding.

It is worthy to note that she chose the right action. The widow could have chosen to pity her situation as opposed to persevering. Which brings me to tell you – be careful that you don't fall into the pit of self-pity.

But Naboth said to Ahab, "The Lord forbid that I should give you the inheritance of my fathers." And Ahab went into his house vexed and sullen because of what Naboth the Jezreelite had said to him, for he had said, "I will not give you the inheritance of my fathers." And he lay down on his bed and turned away his face and would eat no food. (1 Kgs. 21:3-4)

The Scripture I have shared here is a prime example of someone who has allowed self-pity to literally take over his life. Ahab was the king of Israel and could have had absolutely anything he wanted, but when Naboth refused to give up his vineyard, he threw a pity party for himself. So full of himself was the king that he was only made happy again when his wife, the evil Jezebel, set in motion a plan to have Naboth murdered.

Self-pity is an emotional toxin that will literally take over your sense of reasoning and rationality.

Ahab would literally take the life of another man simple to get what he wanted.

I believe self-pity is the absolute worst of spiritual and emotional addictions. People get addicted to this feeling of pity for themselves and the pity that others show them. It literally separates them from reality, which is why they fall into this trap so often. Self-pity will paralyze you from moving forward from the event about which you feel sorry for yourself. Here is what you need to understand:

PERSISTENCE

***You cannot control what happens to you
in life. But you can always choose
whether or not what happens to you
will control you.***

Are you letting what is happening to you dictate the direction of your life? Or are you persevering for the sake of justice and righteousness, like the widow? Do not throw a pity party for yourself. Rather, persevere to the full extent of your ability.

Can't Wait

The reason Jesus painted this judge in such a crude way is because He wanted us to realize that persistence is not always easy.

You are not always going to have people pat you on the back and encourage you along the way. You are not always going to get a trophy and a ribbon to put up in your bedroom, proving that you are persistent. You are going to have to persist through some difficult circumstances where people think you are nothing more than a piece of trash lying by the roadside. They don't care about your needs. They don't care about how you feel. They don't care what you have been through. They are going to tell you to suck it up and move on. Get over it and face the rest of your life like a responsible adult. Quit trying to pursue justice. Quit trying to see the right thing done in life. Just accept the fact that this is the way life is.

Your persistence cannot depend on the affirmation and support of others. Sometimes you have to go it without other people.

Some of you are dealing with that right now. You have people surrounding you that really don't care how things turn out in your life. There is no encouragement. No pat on the back from the people around you.

The Lord is saying you can't wait for someone to come and encourage you. You can't wait for someone to come and tell you what a great job you are doing.

You do have an advocate who is fighting for you.

Consequently, he is able to save to the uttermost those who draw near to God through him, since he always lives to make intercession for them. (Heb. 7:25)

This little woman was all by herself up against a man who had no regard for God. Really, no regard for man either. Yet, because she believed her cause was just, she never gave up. But it was simply because she didn't quit that she received what was right in her life.

So, let me ask you – what are you going to do? Lay there and die? Lay there and give in? Lay there and let the enemy and other people walk all over you? I bet you won't. If you are imitating Christ's character, I bet you won't.

CHAPTER THIRTY-SIX

Three Questions

I have a few questions for you. These are questions that you better have the answers, questions that you had better understand in order to do what you need to be doing for His Kingdom and your life.

The first question is: <u>what are you fighting for?</u> Are you fighting for your family? Are you fighting for your marriage? Are you fighting for your job? Are you fighting for someone in your life who has been wronged? Are you fighting for the calling God has placed upon your life? The calling that others have said will never happen? Are you fighting to get back the vision within you that has seemingly died?

*Whatever it is that you believe in so
deeply that you are not willing to let go,
you need to clearly define what you
are fighting for.*

Clearly define that which you are willing to go up against Goliath and fight even though you are seriously outmanned and outnumbered.

Saying the words is not enough. You can't just say, "I am fighting for my marriage." You have to clearly define what type of marriage you are really fighting for. That way when you go to prayer, you can pray specifically about what you are fighting for.

When David was questioned by his brother about why he was there and why he was fighting, he knew the answer:

> *Now Eliab his eldest brother heard when he spoke to the men. And Eliab's anger was kindled against David, and he said, "Why have you come down? And with whom have you left those few sheep in the wilderness? I know your presumption and the evil of your heart, for you have come down to see the battle." And David said, "What have I done now? Was it not but a word?"* (1 Sam. 17:28-29)

David wasn't fighting <u>against</u> Goliath. He was fighting <u>for</u> the cause of Jehovah.

I think so many times we fight against things, against people, which leads us away from the purpose we are truly fighting for.

This was a penniless and powerless woman staring into the face of a powerful and prosperous judge. Yet, because she had a cause worth fighting for, she was willing to persist until he was willing to give her the justice she deserved.

***In the midst of intense persecution we
must not lose heart but continue to pray
for God's vindication.***

**The second question that you must ask is: <u>why
are you fighting for it?</u>** You can't fight for everything and
not everything is worth fighting for.

There are some people who think they are a mixed
martial artist, and they fight for no other sake than to fight.
This woman was not that kind of person. She was not
fighting just so she could be recognized and lauded as a hero.
She was fighting for her cause. She was fighting for justice.
She was fighting for truth.

Some people take on that warrior mentality just so
other people will notice them. They act out being loud and
fighting for everything without any reasoning behind it.
Which is not what Jesus is calling us to do.

***If you take up a fight just to be noticed,
you will become nothing more than a
contentious person.***

The point is that you should not seek a fight. Rather,
you should fight only when there is an important reason
behind it. In other words – do not create a fight just so you
can fight.

And finally, the third question – <u>how are you going to
fight?</u> Please remember who you are up against.

*For we do not wrestle against flesh and blood,
but against the rulers, against the authorities,*

*against the cosmic powers over this present
darkness, against the spiritual forces of evil in
the heavenly places. (Eph. 6:12)*

You cannot get up and scream and holler and expect this fight to be won. Because this fight is being fought at a spiritual level, not a physical one.

That is the point of why Jesus told this parable.

*And will not God give justice to his elect, who
cry to him day and night? Will he delay long
over them? (Lk. 18:7)*

The judge was unjust, unloving, ungodly, and unrighteous. Still, he gave justice to this woman because of her persistent asking of him. Jesus was saying that if this unjust, unloving, ungodly, unrighteous judge will give this penniless and powerless woman what she needs, how much more will a just, loving, righteous, and eternal heavenly Father give to those who persistently ask Him what they need?

Look to the Gospel of Mark:

*Truly, I say to you, whoever does not receive the
kingdom of God like a child shall not enter it."*
(Mk. 10:15)

What a fantastic message this is. It is a message telling believers not to overcomplicate things but to simplify. Receive the Kingdom of God and all that He will do with simplistic understanding of a child.

I want to challenge you today to start living like a child again. I have a young son, and we have our special time together (just he and I) each week where we do something fun. And in that time, I never – not once – have brought up the fact that our national debt is like thirty trillion dollars. Just as I have never brought up the unemployment rate or even the 2020 presidential election. In fact, when my boy and I spend time together as father and son, he acts like he doesn't have a care in the world. Do you know why? Because he is not even a teenager yet. So, he really doesn't have a care.

When I tucked him into bed the other night then went and laid in my own, I realized that my son fully expects to wake up to a nice breakfast, clean clothes, more than enough toys to play with, and most of all, a family who loves him unconditionally. As I contemplated all of this, I think I understand a little more what Jesus meant when He said that we are to receive the Kingdom of God as a child. He uses the smallest and most unnoticed of all in the human race, a little child, to illustrate the powerful truths of the Kingdom.

What I want to point out to you is that those who are successful in their walk with God and in life have never forgotten how to be a child.

I challenge you today to begin to trust God like a young child trusts their parents. Live with the faith and imagination of a child. I believe you will find yourself in a spiritual position of confidence and faith that will make the Kingdom of God more real to you than it has ever been before.

CHAPTER THIRTY-SEVEN

What Is Your Plan

So, what is your plan? What will you do now that you are unlocking the mysteries of God's Kingdom?

Maybe you know what the next step is. Maybe you are not all that sure. No matter which it is, I have something God wants you to do. It is the last element (that I will refer to) regarding your confidence. That last element is that you must learn to pray with confidence.

And this is the confidence that we have toward him, that if we ask anything according to his will he hears us. (1 Jn. 5:14)

The meaning of the word <u>confidence</u> in the Greek refers to freedom in speaking, unreservedness in speech. To speak openly, frankly, without ambiguity.

So, to pray with confidence to our Father means to pray knowing that He hears us and helps us. After all, we are to have faith that we will possess what we pray for if it is God's will and for His good.

Now faith is the assurance of things hoped for, the conviction of things not seen. (Heb. 11:1)

So, I urge you to pray as if it has already happened and to pray without ceasing (1 Thess. 5:17).

There was an athletics coach who was known for posting signs throughout the locker room to motivate his players to play at a higher level of excellence. One sign was hung on the door as they left the locker room and went on to the playing field. The sign read: "Discipline is not what I do TO you, it is what I do FOR you."

Too many times, when we hear the word **discipline** we have a negative connotation about it. Creating disciplines in our life is something God does <u>FOR</u> us – not just <u>TO</u> us. One of the most important disciplines for you to develop is that discipline of daily prayer. In fact, in that Scripture to the Thessalonians, Paul instructed the believers at Thessalonica to pray without ceasing. That is an important practice that we need as well. That doesn't mean that you spend twenty-four hours a day in prayer. It simply means that prayer is a perpetual discipline that puts you in a spiritual state where, at any time of the day, you are ready to pray.

> *I encourage you to examine your prayer life. Ask yourself if prayer is a daily discipline you exercise. Is it a discipline that makes you spiritually strong and ready to obey what God commands?*

Make time to pray because if you don't make time to pray, you will never have time to pray. And prayer is essential to a believer's life and to your heavenly Father.

CHAPTER THIRTY-EIGHT

Another Parable

He put another parable before them, saying, "The kingdom of heaven is like a grain of mustard seed that a man took and sowed in his field. It is the smallest of all seeds, but when it has grown it is larger than all the garden plants and becomes a tree, so that the birds of the air come and make nests in its branches." (Mt. 13:31-32)

The disciples had come to believe that Jesus was indeed the Messiah, the King of kings.

This parable of the mustard seed added more information about the King and the nature of His Kingdom. Even though Jesus' Kingdom would start small, seemingly insignificantly, it would sweep the world. Remember that in the parable of the soils Jesus had said that He was the sower and the field was the "world." He was predicting the amazing breadth of His Kingdom.

Jesus was teaching in this parable that the mustard seed, which is in fact the smallest of field crop seeds, grows to a height of fifteen feet when planted!

ANOTHER PARABLE

While Jesus was there in Israel with only a handful of disciples at the time he gave them this parable, the prophets in Psalm 72:8-11 had declared this about the extent of the Messiah's Kingdom:

May he have dominion from sea to sea,
and from the River to the ends of the earth!
May desert tribes bow down before him,
and his enemies lick the dust! May the kings of
Tarshish and of the coastlands render him
tribute; may the kings of Sheba and Seba bring
gifts! May all kings fall down before him, all
nations serve him!

While moving through the subject of how we are to be representatives of the Kingdom of God to the world, I was reminded of the story of a woman named Martha Berry. She was born just outside the town of Rome, Georgia in the year 1866. She was born into a wealthy family that owned a vast estate in that area. She asked for a playhouse and her father had a cabin built for her.

One Sunday, as she was studying her Bible in the cabin, Martha Berry heard the voices of children outside. She went out and saw some of the poor children from nearby Possum Trot playing. Miss Berry was a teenager by this time, and she called the children to her and began to entertain and educate them by telling them stories of the Bible.

Her Bible classes met each week in her playhouse. She taught children that would never have had the opportunity to go to school. She taught them how to read and write. She taught them arithmetic and other lessons. Then, in 1902, she had the idea to start a boy's school nearby Lavender Mountain. She deeded land, raised funds, and opened the doors to students, and the Berry Industrial School for Boys was formed. The school continued to grow, adding a program for girls.

Today, if you were to visit Rome, Georgia, you can still visit the house that Martha Berry lived in until she died. You can also see the cabin playhouse where she taught the poor children about the love of God. If you visit Rome, Georgia, you can also see what I would call a "mustard seed" school as well as what it has become.

That little, seemingly insignificant school has become Berry College, which sits on 28,000 beautiful acres of Georgia real estate. There are 38 major buildings and well over two thousand students. Berry College is widely recognized as one of the outstanding comprehensive colleges in the southern U.S.

This school that began in the humblest of ways has been a blessing to tens of thousands of young people and students from thirty-seven states and nine countries.

I tell you this story because, through this parable, I believe Jesus is teaching us that what starts off small may have far-reaching results. Jesus was teaching His followers what the Kingdom of God is like. He was trying to teach them how we, as ambassadors to the Kingdom of God, are to represent His Kingdom. I believe this parable is one of the most powerful kinds because it illustrates that what the world would deem as small and insignificant, what the world would most likely reject and not even pay attention to is growing even today in a world-wide movement in which

ANOTHER PARABLE

Christ is worshipped as the King of kings and the Lord of lords.

CHAPTER THIRTY-NINE

Small Beginnings

***Never discount small beginnings because
in the Kingdom of God, small beginnings
often lead to supernatural endings.***

The beauty of the parables is that Jesus started with something they could understand and moved to something they did not understand. He started with something natural and moved to something supernatural. He started with what is material and moved to what is spiritual. He started with what is simple and moved to what is profound.

So, when He compared the Kingdom of God to the grain of a mustard seed, the disciples knew exactly what He was talking about. While the mustard seed is not the smallest seed known to man, it was the smallest seed planted in the gardens of Jesus' day. The mustard seed itself is very tiny. It takes about seven hundred and fifty of them to make up a single gram. There are twenty-eight grams in an ounce. That would mean that there are some 21,000 mustard seeds in an ounce.

What is so incredible about this tiny seed is that when planted in the right soil, it produces an incredibly large tree.

Something very large comes from something so small. And that's the point.

> *The greatest among you shall be your servant. Whoever exalts himself will be humbled, and whoever humbles himself will be exalted. (Mt. 23:11-12)*

The word of God has a completely different definition of what greatness means. We live in a world where position, title, and authority mean everything, a world where it is all about how you look, who you know, the type of car you own, or the kind of house in which you live. The world judges people based on the color of their skin, the type of clothes they wear, the level of education they possess. We live in a world whose criteria for greatness flies in the face of what Jesus taught us about people and the world around us.

If we are not careful, even within the church, we can begin to possess that same mindset. I believe the Kingdom that Jesus is building began in the most obscure and seemingly insignificant ways...

Jesus was born in the obscure town of Bethlehem in abject poverty.

> *But you, O Bethlehem Ephrathah, who are too little to be among the clans of Judah, from you shall come forth for me one who is to be ruler in Israel, whose coming forth is from of old, from ancient days. (Mic. 5:2)*

He was raised in Nazareth of Galilee, a town considered to be wicked and worldly by the Jews. Nobody believed anything good would come out of Nazareth.

Nathanael said to him, "Can anything good come out of Nazareth?" Philip said to him, "Come and see." (Jn. 1:46)
They replied, "Are you from Galilee too? Search and see that no prophet arises from Galilee."
(Jn. 7:52)

He had no money. He had no support from the religious leaders of the day. Jesus was considered to be a nobody from nowhere who would amount to nothing. His followers were, for the most part, the dregs of society. The people He grew up with in His hometown rejected Him. He was despised and rejected by many men. The Romans eventually nailed Him to a cross and buried Him in a tomb that He could not even afford.

If you were to look at the resume of Jesus today, most would discount it as a resume of a man who was insignificant and unsuccessful.

He lost as many followers as He gained because His message was hard to swallow. One of His best friends and closest followers betrayed Him into the hands of the Roman government. Another one of His best friends cursed and swore that He had never even known who He was. The men in whom He invested three and a half years of training, when He was arrested and needed them, all ran away from Him and stayed in hiding. They didn't even stand with Him during His trial.

Yet, in the midst of all this seemingly insignificant and unsuccessful resume of a ministry, you have the Son of God who has built a universal church by transforming people into believers from every single continent in the world. From every tribe, tongue, and nation in the world, He has built a force that cannot be reckoned with. It is one which cannot be destroyed by the enemy. It is a church that will live on throughout all of eternity when every other organization and government entity has passed off the scene, fulfilling exactly what He said He would do.

> *And I tell you, you are Peter, and on this rock I will build my church, and the gates of hell shall not prevail against it.* (Mt. 16:18)

At the time of His ministry, I don't believe anyone could see that the tiny seed Jesus was sowing would become this universal church that cannot be silenced and cannot be stopped.

In the beginning, there was only a ragtag group of followers and Jesus. His followers consisted of some uneducated fishermen, a few revolutionaries, some women, and a traitor. Even by the time the day of Pentecost came around, after His death and marvelous resurrection, there were still only one hundred and twenty devoted followers of Jesus' way. That's after three and a half years of evangelizing and teaching!

Then something monumental happened. On the day of Pentecost, a spark ignited a flame. When the Holy Spirit fell on those believers and the disciples were baptized in the Holy Ghost, the same man who just a few weeks before had cursed and sworn that he had never even meet Jesus, let alone followed Him – this man stood and preached because he had seen the risen Lord and what a game changer that became.

A New Way

When the Holy Spirit fell upon the followers of Christ the day of Pentecost, a wave of change went out across the land.

So those who received his word were baptized,
and there were added that day about three
thousand souls. (Acts 2:41)

Three thousand souls! Remember that in three and a half years, Jesus' total followers amounted to about one hundred and twenty. In a few moment's time, it grew to three thousand! And if that wasn't great enough, a short time later another five thousand were saved at one time.

But many of those who had heard the word
believed, and the number of the men came to
about five thousand. (Acts 4:4)

The church began to grow at an astounding rate. It wasn't many days until the church in Jerusalem was said to have numbered some fifty thousand people! This was just the beginning. As the message was carried around the world, vast multitudes began to come to Jesus.

So great was the spread of the gospel that it was said to have turned the world upside down.

And when they could not find them, they
dragged Jason and some of the brothers before
the city authorities, shouting, "These men who
have turned the world upside down have
come here also..." (Acts 17:6)

This amazing growth has not stopped. It has continued from that point until today. Who but God knows the true count of souls that have been saved from sin and damnation? Everywhere the gospel seed has been planted, souls have been saved and lives have been changed. The church has continued to grow and the Kingdom of God on earth has continued to expand.

What is even greater than this truth is the one that there will come a day when a vast multitude that cannot be numbered will stand before the Lord in heaven and praise Him for saving them by His grace. We will have a chance to show that we are listening.

After this I looked, and behold, a great multitude
that no one could number, from every nation,
from all tribes and peoples and languages,
standing before the throne and before the
Lamb, clothed in white robes, with palm
branches in their hands... (Rev. 7:9)

And to think that it all began with Jesus; it began with a seemingly insignificant band of disciples.

Small Beginnings

God has a way of bringing great things out of small beginnings. Look at David in the Old Testament. He was a mustard seed. Don't think so? Look at the facts of David's life.

He was the youngest of Jesse's eight boys. He was ignored and given the job that no one else in the family wanted, which was sitting on a hillside taking care of the sheep. When God called Samuel to anoint the new king out of the house of Jesse, David wasn't even invited to the party. Jesse didn't even think he was worth being considered.

Yet, God took this "mustard seed" of a man and made a giant-killing king out of him. David has gone down in history as one of the greatest kings of Israel. This, there can be no dispute about. Yet he was only a tiny seed sown by God.

Another tiny seed is a man named Gideon. He was considered the weakest man in the weakest clan of Israel. He was living in a spiritually backslidden nation and, even more than that, he was living in an adulterous backslidden family who was the poorest in the region. But God took this "mustard seed" and made him into a military genius, defeating 135,000 Midianites with a mere three hundred men.

> ***God can take someone who seems insignificant and make something truly great out of them.***

God can take a little red-headed boy nobody wanted on their team and make him a great leader in the second world war, which is what He did with Winston Churchill. God can take a backward stuttering man and use him to lead Israel out of bondage and bring the Law of God to humanity, which is what He did with Moses. God can even take an awkward, shy shoe salesman and use him to shake up the world for Jesus, as He did with D.L. Moody.

What About You

The question is, what can God do with your life? I pose this question to you because you may have a mustard seed beginning in your life.

According to the Bible, you were a sinner.

*For all have sinned and fall short of the glory
of God... (Rom. 3:23)*

According to the Bible, you were under a death sentence and you were headed to hell.

*For the wages of sin is death, but the free gift of
God is eternal life in Christ Jesus our Lord.
(Rom. 6:23)*

But also, according to the Bible, you are made alive by Jesus and made to sit in heavenly places with the Almighty.

*But God, being rich in mercy, because of the
great love with which he loved us, even when we
were dead in our trespasses, made us alive
together with Christ—by grace you have been
saved—and raised us up with him and seated us*

with him in the heavenly places in Christ Jesus, so that in the coming ages he might show the immeasurable riches of his grace in kindness toward us in Christ Jesus. For by grace you have been saved through faith. And this is not your own doing; it is the gift of God.
(Eph. 2:4-8)

God placed you in the body of Christ so you could bear the fruit you were created to bear for the glory of God.

It doesn't matter how you begin. It only matters how you finish. Some people may be so focused on how they began their lives that they lose their focus on how God wants them to finish their lives. They are so focused on where they have been that they lose sight of where they are going. They spend all of their time looking behind them when they should be looking out in front of them. If this is you, then it is time to start acting on or resuming your service for God. To help with this, I will describe three things that, when implemented in your life, will help you develop into whatever it is God urges you to be.

Be Planted

To grow, you must first be planted.

Action point #1: <u>You must be planted.</u>

*He put another parable before them,
saying, "The kingdom of heaven is like a grain of
mustard seed that a man took and
sowed in his field." (Mt. 13:31)*

When the tiny mustard seed is planted in good soil, it germinates and produces a very large shrub-like plant that eventually grows into something that looks like a tree. Some mustard plants have been known to grow as high as fifteen feet tall.

Think about that. A fifteen foot tall tree coming from a seed that weighs one-seven hundred and fiftieth of a gram. Something so small, with such humble beginnings, can become something that is truly amazing is, well... amazing.

The lesson here is that there is no limit to what God can do in your life when you are planted in the right soil. Meaning that when you are put in a right position, there's always an opportunity for growth. you can always prosper.

Yet, here is the thing – being planted in the right soil and the right environment first means <u>being planted</u>.

The seed that is never planted is the seed that will never produce. The growing of the seed is completely dependent on the sowing of the seed.

***Don't expect to grow if you
are unwilling to sow.***

That is why, if we expect God to do great things in our lives, we cannot continually bring to Him our need. We have to continually bring to Him our seed.

***The reason many people never grow into
who God has designed for them to be is
because they are more interested in
bringing their <u>need</u> over
bringing their seed.***

Let God plant you where you were created to be planted. Let Him plant you into the correct *environment* where you can be the most fruitful.

This may be a message meant specifically for you. So, listen closely, the problem is not the seed within you. But it is the fact that you have not been planted or are planted in the wrong place. It just might be that you are planted in the wrong environment. Or you are planted around the wrong people.

Think about it. You can have good seed, but if it is planted in bad soil then it will not grow properly.

BE PLANTED

Truly, truly, I say to you, unless a grain of
wheat falls into the earth and dies, it remains
alone; but if it dies, it bears much fruit.
(Jn. 12:24)

The seed has to die to its current status (yourself) so it can become something greater than it already is.

I am here to remind you that within you
lies the seed of greatness, which is a
product of God's grace. And also, to
inform you that if you are living in the
grace of God then the greatness
of God lives within you.

Be Positive

Your perspective is relevant. Some do not believe this to be a solid truth. I can assure you it is.

Action point #2: <u>You must be positive.</u>

You cannot minimize what God can do within you. Do not be like those people who minimize themselves by what they say, how they think, and how they live.

Because what you do, think, believe, and say directs you towards what will and will not happen in your life.

If you really believe that you have the seed of the Kingdom within you, you must behave like you do.

There is a reason that verse six in the fourth chapter of Colossians references our speech. It is because our Lord urges us to speak carefully, rightly, so that we will continue towards a fruitful life.

Let your speech always be gracious, seasoned with salt, so that you may know how you ought to answer each person. (Col. 4:6)

We must never underestimate the *power* of the words we speak. Too many people carelessly throw words around as if they have no effect on the world around us. But little do we realize the emotions evoked in not only our hearts but also the hearts of others who hear those words.

> ***My point is simple: be aware of the power your words have on you and on other people.***

Work hard at trying to utilize God's words as your words. Speak His verses over your lives. Also be certain that your intention is to edify and encourage the people to whom you speak. Words matter, so choose them with wisdom.

CHAPTER FORTY-FIVE

Produce

Action point #3: <u>You must produce.</u>

Look at what the seed of the grace of God has done to the world:

> *It is the smallest of all seeds, but when it has*
> *grown it is larger than all the garden plants and*
> *becomes a tree, so that the birds of the air come*
> *and make nests in its branches.* (Mt. 13:32)

This tiny seed grew into an immense plant. Its branches spread themselves abroad, offering a place for the birds to rest. In the shadow of that plant the birds found shelter from the storms, rest from their weariness, and shade from the heat of the sun.

This humble seed produced a plant that gave rest and shelter to the birds of the air the humble mustard seed produced a plant that had many uses among the human community as well. People gathered its leaves and served them as food. The seeds were crushed and used as a condiment; the pungent flavor enhanced the bland diet of the people. Those seeds also were used as medicine; they were crushed and mixed with other things to make antidotes for snake, scorpion, and spider bites.

Just as the plant in this parable brought shelter to the birds, so the Kingdom of God has provided shelter for those who have turned to Jesus.

Everywhere the gospel has germinated, compassion, decency, and morality have sprung up. Hospitals and schools have been founded. Everywhere the gospel has been preached, it has brought about the destruction of demonism, cannibalism, polygamy, child sacrifice, and heathenism. The spread of the gospel has inspired orphanages for the fatherless and homes for the homeless to be built. The gospel has reached out to comfort the bereaved, care for the infirm, and care for the sick. The gospel has changed individuals, communities, and nations. Even the United States of America owes its existence and blessings to the spread of the gospel of God's grace.

This nation was founded on the principles of the gospel and the Christian faith. Even those who reject the gospel in America today still reap the benefits of a nation founded by God and for God.

When the Kingdom of God moves in with divine power, the kingdom of Satan must fall before its appearance. It may have humble beginnings, but God has used it to accomplish great and wonderful things.

Why do I tell you all of that? Because Jesus said:

PRODUCE

*Nor will they say, 'Look, here it is!' or 'There!' for
behold, the kingdom of God is in the midst
of you.* (Lk. 17:21)

We, as ambassadors to the Kingdom, are to proclaim
the gospel with faithfulness so that others can come into the
shelter that the Kingdom provides.

**Step into being the person God has
predestined you to be. Be that thing that
others can find rest, shelter, and
provisions through.**

CHAPTER FORTY-SIX

Seek Your Purpose

At the outset of this book, I declared how Jesus Christ has a purpose for your life. Part of that purpose is your being an ambassador for His Kingdom. Then all throughout the book, I have referenced several of the Lord's parables, containing the hidden and incredible truths that He used as teaching tools. Now, to end this material I want to give another nugget. I want to give you a way to do more for yourself and others. And to do this I'm going to provide you with ten helpful "steps" to help you step into the miraculous with Jesus.

Let's begin with the story of Peter and John meeting a lame man at the gate called Beautiful. Most of you are familiar with this story. It is a well-known miraculous feat, one many people can relate to. Because, like this man, they feel as if they are never going to have the ability to get up from where they are and move forward to where they want to be. I am, of course, describing the events found in Acts 3.

You may feel like that crippled man, stuck in life, as if your life is the way it is always going to be and there's no getting around it. But I'm here to tell you that with Jesus in your life, things begin to change. When Jesus walks in the room, the whole situation changes.

It is because Jesus affects every single aspect of your life. This means that He affects both the physical and spiritual areas of your life. This is why the enemy hates it when you let Jesus into your life. It is because He has dominion over every spirit.

Every spirit of the enemy trembles when Jesus walks into the room.

When Jesus walks into the room, the spirit of infirmity knows that the Great Physician is there. When Jesus walks into the room, the spirit of oppression knows that the Great Deliverer has arrived. When Jesus walks into the room, the spirit of depression and anxiety knows the Prince of Peace has made His appearance. Understand that, just as He gives His lessons to you, so too will He display His presence in your life.

God is sovereign. Therefore, why wouldn't a person want a Sovereign God on his side? The word "sovereign" comes from the Latin word "super." It conveys the ideas of superior and supreme, primary and paramount, unequaled and unexcelled. The God of the Bible is eternal and self-existent. He is supreme in excellence and perfect in all his ways. He is the one and only autonomous being who is self-controlled, with the right and power of self-government. God is infinite in His imperial independence. His capacities and capabilities far surpass the scope of human reasons. God does keep his promises because they are holy and true. That's a fact of reality that you can count on!

Ten Steps

Now Peter and John were going up to the temple at the hour of prayer, the ninth hour. And a man lame from birth was being carried, whom they laid daily at the gate of the temple that is called the Beautiful Gate to ask alms of those entering the temple. Seeing Peter and John about to go into the temple, he asked to receive alms. And Peter directed his gaze at him, as did John, and said, "Look at us." And he fixed his attention on them, expecting to receive something from them. But Peter said, "I have no silver and gold, but what I do have I give to you. In the name of Jesus Christ of Nazareth, rise up and walk!" And he took him by the right hand and raised him up, and immediately his feet and ankles were made strong. And leaping up, he stood and began to walk, and entered the temple with them, walking and leaping and praising God. And all the people saw him walking and praising God, and recognized him as the one who sat at the Beautiful Gate of the temple, asking for alms. And they were filled

*with wonder and amazement at what had
happened to him.* (Acts 3:1-10)

This story is what is called narrative writing. Narrative is one of many styles of literature that appears in the Bible. In narrative writing not every detail contains a principle that is to be a reproduced in the life of every disciple, but can.

There are many things that are recorded in the narrative portions of the Bible that are definitely not intended by God to be repeatable events. For example, the book of Exodus narrates the story about how Moses led Israel out of Egypt through the sea. Stephen was stoned to death for placing his trust in Christ. The Apostle Paul was shipwrecked because he was faithfully following God. I could give you a list of about 2000 examples of this from the Bible. But in some other cases, narrative writing may be replicated; such as this instance between Peter and John.

1. **<u>The Step of Agreement</u>** – Peter and John went up together to the temple.

Peter and John were not simply out on a leisurely stroll for no reason. They probably actually had a discussion in which they came to an agreement of some kind to go to the temple daily to pray. It was probably what they did every day. They probably just got up and left for prayer without any further discussion about their routine at all because they'd already came into an agreement as to what they were going to do daily.

They were looking to perform the will of the Lord, to pray. They were in agreement with one another to continue the work that Jesus had been doing. Then when they came across this lame man, they were in agreement to perform a miraculous work on him. Which was certainly possible because look at what is said in Matthew 18:

Again I say to you, if two of you agree on earth about anything they ask, it will be done for them by my Father in heaven. (Mt. 18:19)

2. <u>The Step of Timing</u>

Now Peter and John were going up to the temple at the hour of prayer, the ninth hour. (Acts 3:1)

When did Peter and John go to the temple? At the ninth hour when it was prayer time. In other words, when there would be an abundance of people.

If you are trying to find people who need help or if you are looking for people of faith then going to a place of worship at the time of worship is a pretty good idea. Their timing was important. Just as your timing when wanting to do work for God's Kingdom is important.

3. <u>The Step of Persistence</u>

Persistence is key in most everything in life. Wouldn't you agree?

When did the crippled man's friends of family put the man at the gate called Beautiful? The same place they had always placed him, just as they did every day.

... whom they laid daily...

Eventually it was their daily routine to place this man right there each day, which definitely displayed persistence.

4. **The Step of Access**

It was just pointed out that for someone to help you or for you to help others means having access to one another. What better place for this man to receive help or support from the people than at one of the many gates leading in and out of the city. In the end, the lame man received healing because Peter and John had access to him. Had he been in his home, they would not have found him.

5. **The Step of Focus**

And Peter directed his gaze at him, as did John,
and said, "Look at us." (Acts 3:4)

It wasn't that Peter was just going to provide his healing. Peter also knew that in this instance, the man's entire focus needed to be on the power of God that was within him. Why? Well Jesus did come onto the scene working miracles, but there had not been miracles in Israel for centuries. There were no prophets in Israel in the first century before Jesus' arrival. God had been silent for 400 years. Jesus' miracles were a dramatic intervention of God into the affairs of men in Palestine, and they were for the purpose of authenticating his role as Messiah.

The apostles' healing miracles were similar in purpose to those of Jesus, they were authenticating. Their purpose was a divine stamp of approval upon them so that their message would be accepted as coming from God, not from their own minds. Therefore, if he lost his focus, if he became distracted by the people around him, he may have missed out on the miracle that God wanted to bring into his life.

There are people who are missing God's work in their life because they have become so distracted by what is around them. Maybe this someone is you.

When you are distracted, you lose the direction of where you desire to go. You know how this goes. If you are walking toward a landmark, the best way for you to reach that landmark is to keep your eyes focused on where you are going.

My advice is that you keep the promise of God right in front of you at all times.

If you are believing God for healing your body, and He has promised healing to you, then why not visualize yourself healed. See yourself walking free from cancer, walking free from pain. If you are believing God for a new job, and He has promised a new job to you, why not start acting as if you already have the job. If God has promised you something, you should keep that promise right in front of you. If you need to take a picture of the house you are believing God for, and He has promised a new house to you, then why not take a picture of it and paste it in your journal and look at it every day.

Your faith is going to move you in the direction of your focus. Whatever captures your focus will either feed your faith or starve it. The only way to increase your faith is to change what you are focused on.

The reason so many people don't receive anything from God is because they are so focused on what they <u>don't</u> have that they never learn to focus on what they <u>can</u> have.

The more you talk about how you lack financially, it always seems that the more you end up lacking financially. The more you talk about how depressed you are, it always seems that you become more depressed.

Never forget this: you can either say what you have, or you can have what you say.

So instead of talking about what you don't have, start talking about what you can have. Instead of talking about what you can't do, start talking about what you can do. After all:

I can do all things through him who strengthens me. (Phil. 4:13)

I'll say it again: your faith is going to move you in the direction of your focus.

Whatever you look at the longest becomes the strongest. This means that your focus will reveal what is in your heart. Therefore, change your focus and you will change the direction of your faith.

There is power in focus.

I know that there are so many of you out there who would be able to do more, receive more, and be more if only you would change your focus. If you would just change what you are thinking about, change what you are talking about.

Why is this true? Because you change what you expect.

6. <u>**The Step of Expectancy**</u>

*And he fixed his attention on them, expecting to
receive something from them.* (Acts 3:5)

When Peter convinced the lame man to change his focus from merely receiving alms, that was when his future changed for the better. Yes, this man changed his focus and focused on the person who could help him with something so much better. Something rose up within him and suddenly he began to expect something to happen.

Now, it could have been that he expected Peter and John to throw a few coins into his beggar's jar. Or he could have expected something beyond that. The Scripture is not clear. It merely says he expected to receive something from them.

> ***When you refine your focus on God
> instead of the daily distraction of
> everything and everyone else around
> you, suddenly an expectation will begin
> to rise within you.***

This can happen when your faith is not distracted by the comments, opinions, or doubts of others. Your focus then begins to elevate to a new level because you are trusting in the Lord. And it is that new level of expectation that will unlock the door for God's presence in your life.

It is not only you that are wanting a union with God. He too is looking for those people willing to live in a spirit of expectation. As described in Matthew 9:

> *When he entered the house, the blind men came*
> *to him, and Jesus said to them, "Do you believe*
> *that I am able to do this?" They said to him,*
> *"Yes, Lord." Then he touched their eyes,*
> *saying, "According to your faith be it*
> *done to you." (Mt. 9:28-29)*

The truth is that God often meets you at your level of expectation.

This man in Acts 3 was fully convinced he was going to get something from Peter and John. He didn't know what, but he was going to get something. He knew this because these men took the time to stop and engage him in conversation. They told him to look at them and not look at anyone else. Why would they do that unless there was something they had to give him? So, he looked up.

> *And he fixed his attention on them, expecting to*
> *receive something from them. (Acts 3:5)*

He paid attention to them because he knew that they had something to give.

What would happen if we would all become like this man? I'll tell you what. We would give heed to the conversation in which God has engaged us. Be convinced, not just hope for, not a maybe so, but be thoroughly convinced that you are not leaving this place until you receive something from God. We would step into the position and perform the work we are made to do.

To *expect* something means to be convinced or even hope that it is going to happen. There's no avoiding it. The hope that is within you is inevitable. Which results in a fantastic thing – it means there is no room for doubt because expectation fills you up.

> *But let him ask in faith, with no doubting, for the one who doubts is like a wave of the sea that is driven and tossed by the wind. For that person must not suppose that he will receive anything from the Lord; he is a double-minded man, unstable in all his ways. (Jms. 1:6-8)*

7. <u>**The Step of Support**</u>

> *But Peter said, "I have no silver and gold, but what I do have I give to you. In the name of Jesus Christ of Nazareth, rise up and walk!" And he took him by the right hand and raised him up, and immediately his feet and ankles were made strong. (Acts 3:6-7)*

Those who perform for the Kingdom of God have a strong support system around them.

Peter knew this man had never walked a day in his life. He knew that for him to just simply say stand up, this man's mind would be full of questions.

Imagine the thoughts of this man the moment that Peter was raising him to his feet and was about to let go. I have little doubt that this man had some thoughts along the lines of, "This fool is about to let go of me and I'm going to fall to the ground like a bag of trash. Doesn't he know that I have never stood on my legs, ever? What if I fall down? What will it be like when people laugh at me? What if I try to walk but I am not able to and I fall on my face?"

But when Peter reached out his hand and took the hand of the man who was getting ready to walk for the very first time of his life, he was letting this man know that they were in this thing together. I am not simply going to pray for you and let you do this on your own.

> ***I am going to pray for you and then lift you up through your time of doubt and fear. I am here to support you. I am here to help you. I am here to get you started on this new journey as a man who has been healed.***

I believe Peter knew that if this man would merely take the first step, the second step would be easier. Then the third step would be even easier than that. He just needed someone to help him take the first step.

> ***As the body of Christ, we have got to get better at supporting each other as we take the steps into our position within the Kingdom of God.***

There are so many people who are in need of a helping hand. Yet, too many times we simply say, "I am praying for you," and then walk away. They just might need you to hold out your hand and tell them: "Come on, let's take that first step together. Let's pray together. Let's stand together."

When you support someone else in taking their step into the Kingdom, know that it will come back to you. One day, God will send someone to support you when you need to take steps into a higher position for His Kingdom.

One of the values our churches need to have is the value of community. We should be a community of believers who values every individual regardless of their current status or background.

I truly believe it is a strong sense of community that will bring growth into not only your life but also into your church. I say this because people in this world are looking for a group of believers who are serious about supporting each other as they chase God's best in their individual lives. I think it is fair to say that many people are tired of walking into churches only to be shot down through criticism and judgmental attitudes.

So, I said all of that to say this: the church needs to be a place of support. It needs to be a place where people can come and be built up, not torn down. It needs to be a place that supports Paul's declaration to the people of Ephesus:

*Let no corrupting talk come out of your mouths,
but only such as is good for building up,
as fits the occasion, that it may give grace to
those who hear. (Eph. 4:29)*

8. <u>The Step of Progression</u>

*And leaping up, he stood and began to walk,
and entered the temple with them, walking and
leaping and praising God. (Acts 3:8)*

The result of the man being healed was understandable and dramatic; he "stood, then walked, then he leaped." Notice the progression in this work (miracle) for the Kingdom. First of all, he stood, then walked, then he leaped.

He didn't jump up and start running around like a crazy man. Recall that this man had never walked a single step a day in his life. Sometimes the things performed for the Almighty happen in a progressive manner. It may not be an instantaneous healing. It may be a progressive healing. It may not be an instantaneous deliverance. It may be a progressive deliverance.

*And he took the blind man by the hand and led
him out of the village, and when he had spit on
his eyes and laid his hands on him, he asked
him, "Do you see anything?" And he looked up
and said, "I see people, but they look like trees,
walking." Then Jesus laid his hands on his eyes
again; and he opened his eyes, his sight was*

restored, and he saw everything clearly.
(Mk. 8:23-25)

You may know exactly what I am referring to. You may be **in the process** of something for God right now. If you do not see it (whatever it is) playing out instantly before your eyes, understand that that doesn't mean it is not going to happen.

> ***Just because the answer hasn't come doesn't mean you stop asking. Just because the door has not flown open does not mean you stop knocking. Just because you haven't found what you are looking for doesn't mean you stop looking.***

It's a process. You don't walk away when there are no instantaneous results. So, don't just give up at the beginning of the process. Understand that the answer is on the way.

9. <u>The Principle of Visibility</u>

And all the people saw him walking and praising God... (Acts 3:9)

Think about if you were this man for just a moment. You have never walked a day in your life. You have been lame from the day you were born. Even in your mother's womb, your lameness didn't come through disease or accident. There was nothing external that caused you to be handicapped. So, your entire life has been spent watching other people do what you would love to do. As a young boy, you watched other boys run and play. You watched as friends walked strong all the while you simply laid there. As you grew up, you watched others work hard and earn a living. All the while, you were confined to sitting by the gate of the temple begging for just enough to get by for that day.

Then suddenly you are miraculously healed and able to do what you have always longed to do. Suddenly the ankles that have never had the ability to support the weight of your body are strong. Your legs can now carry you where you want to go. Suddenly, you have the ability to walk without anyone helping you. Now, how do you think you are going to react? You are going to make sure everybody knows what just happened to you. You are going to walk right up to those who looked down on you or laughed at you or belittled you. You are going to run up to those people who said you were never going to change. You are going to make sure that they all know the change that this man made possible in your life.

The point is this: when you walk in the Kingdom of God, you might just want the world to know and hopefully you want the world to walk in it with you.

Can I tell you that today is a great day for you? I don't mean to sound like a snake charmer. But I know that today is a great time for you because today needs to be the day you start making a change, the kind of change that gives the world the right kind of example of what it means to be an ambassador for God's Kingdom.

Understand that the world needs to know Jesus is still working.

He still heals the sick. He delivers those who are drug addicted. The Lord is still setting people free from bondage. This is a responsibility that falls partially on the shoulders of His people. Why? Because there is no reason for us to go to church and worship the Lord every week just to keep that miraculous or providential work to ourselves. We have the answers that the world is looking for. They just don't know it.

So, go out and tell someone about God's presence in your life.

Tell someone about your miracle, what God has done for you. Tell your family the difference God has made in your life. Tell the world about Jesus and His many stories. Then help them understand their need for God's saving work in their lives.

Good or bad, the world today responds to what they see. They need to see a change in the lives of others. They don't simply need to hear about it. They need to see it. Show them the miracles that Jesus is making happen in your life.

Do you know why they need to see the miraculous?

Because the miraculous points them to the miracle worker – Jesus Christ Himself. Which leads me to my tenth step...

10. <u>The Step of Praise</u>

...and recognized him as the one who sat at the Beautiful Gate of the temple, asking for alms.

TEN STEPS

And they were filled with wonder and
amazement at what had happened to him.
(Acts 3:10)

I think it's safe to say that this was out of the ordinary. These people had gone to the temple every single day. They had gone through the formality of worship and religion. Remember that these were religious people. This man had been sitting right outside of the temple gates. All of that spiritual activity was happening a short distance from him. Still, no real work was done for him. Why?

They had been accustomed to him just simply sitting there day after day and begging for alms. Seeking something to get through (and getting it) but not a thing to help him break through. Why?

It was as if they had gotten so used to just following their routine that they did not bother with certain works.

Does this sound familiar? It should, because some of the world has a bad habit of doing this same thing. God knew this which is one of the reasons that why He gave us this story.

Here is the ugly truth for some:
sometimes people get so accustomed to
going through the motions of going to
work, reading their Bible, and
performing for the Kingdom, that they
seldom take the time to stop and fully
understand that we go to church to
worship the Miracle Worker, that we are
called Christians because we are to do

the things that the Christ Himself has done.

It is past time to recall that every time we gather together, the Miracle Worker, the Lord Jesus Christ, is in our midst.

*For where two or three are gathered in my
name, there am I among them. (Mt. 18:20)*

Which empowers us to execute for Him.

When these people saw the miraculous, it broke them out of their **religious box**. It broke them away from their routine. Put another way, their religious routine was disrupted by the power of God.

Let me just say that I pray daily that my life be disrupted by the power of the Holy Ghost and so should you.

Ask the Lord to give you a divine disruption, one that will jerk you out of your religious rut, a disruption that will take your eyes off of the mundane and turn your gaze towards heavenly things. Ask God to challenge you towards truly serving the living God of the Bible.

*Now to him who is able to do far more
abundantly than all that we ask or
think, according to the power at work within us,
to him be glory in the church and in Christ Jesus
throughout all generations, forever and ever.
Amen. (Eph. 3:20-21)*

The reason that the apostles did the miracle and the reason that Luke told the story is to simply point people to Jesus.

If we keep reading the context, we will see it in what followed:

> *While he clung to Peter and John, all the people, utterly astounded, ran together to them in the portico called Solomon's. And when Peter saw it he addressed the people: "Men of Israel, why do you wonder at this, or why do you stare at us, as though by our own power or piety we have made him walk? The God of Abraham, the God of Isaac, and the God of Jacob, the God of our fathers, glorified his servant Jesus, whom you delivered over and denied in the presence of Pilate, when he had decided to release him.*
> (Acts 3:11-13)

The story was the prelude to what can truly bring the presence of Jesus into anyone's life, the telling of the gospel message that can be the catalyst to eternal salvation. So the miraculous healing always is and was that day to set up the opportunity for the proclamation about Jesus Christ being the Savior.

Salvation Prayer

Is there anything or anyone keeping you from accepting the FREE GIFT of eternal life found in Jesus Christ today? If you believe in the life, death, burial, and resurrection of Jesus, and if you are willing to believe with your heart these five verses of truth, then the eternal life Jesus Christ promised will be yours.

We were all born into—

Sin—Romans 3:23 says:

> *For all have sinned and fall short*
> *of the glory of God.* (NASB)

Sin leads to **death**—Romans 6:23 says:

> *For the wages of sin is death, but the free gift of*
> *God is eternal life in Christ Jesus our Lord.*
> (NASB)

But, it is God's **love** that was demonstrated in the atonement when Jesus Christ was willing to die in our place as a sacrifice for our sin, thus washing away the sin and death from your life.

Romans 5:8 says:

*But God demonstrates His own love toward
us, in that while we were yet sinners,*

Christ died for us. (NASB)

Although God's love is free and available to everyone, not everyone accepts it. So, how do you accept God's love?

By **faith**—Ephesians 2:8-9 says:

*For by grace you have been saved, through
faith; and not of yourselves, it is the [free] gift of
God; not as a result of works, so that no one
may boast.* (NASB)

There's nothing you can do to earn it. But rather, you just have to accept God's love by faith, then you can have **life.** Romans 10:9-10 says:

*If you confess with your moth Jesus as Lord,
and believe in your heart that God raised Him
from the dead, you will be saved; for with the
heart a person believes, resulting in
righteousness, and with the mouth he confesses,
resulting in salvation.* (NASB)

Now, just tell God that you trust His promise about the free gift of forgiveness for the sins in your life. Tell Him thank you for sending His Son Jesus Christ to come and pay a debt that He didn't owe so that you could spend eternity with Him in heaven. If you need a little more direction, you can speak a prayer like this:

Lord, I know that I'm a sinner, but I thank You for Your Son, Jesus Christ, who died on the cross for my sins and rose on the third day so that I could be forgiven and spend eternity with You in heaven. I now freely accept His sacrifice and am asking You to please send Your Holy Spirit to indwell with me all the days of my life to direct me, to help me along the way of life, and to help me know You better. Thank You. In Jesus' name, I pray. Amen.

If you truly meant what you just prayed, the Bible says in 2 Corinthians 5:17 that you are now a **new creature**:

Therefore, if anyone is in Christ, he is a new creature; the old things have passed away; behold, new things have come. (NASB)

Going forward, you may feel different, or you may not. Emotions often follow and indicate a change of heart. However, it is God's Word and the Holy Spirit that gives the assurance that you belong to Him (Romans 8:16).

The most important thing is that your sins have now been forgiven through faith in Jesus Christ and all that He has done. You now have the FREE gift of salvation and eternal life with Him. You have been set free from the "old things" (sin) to live this new life in Christ. You now have a new heart and a new Spirit living within you. This may be a little hard to comprehend right now, but with time and understanding it will become clearer. To be that new disciple of Christ means that you abandon your "old" life to embrace a "new" life with Him.

I'd like to thank Dr. Kyle Lance Martin & Time to Revive for these salvation notes, which were modified and used with permission.

Deliverance Prayer

Dear Heavenly Father, I come to You now in Jesus' name, to repent of all the sins in my life and also in the lives of my ancestors that may have resulted in a curse from the enemy against me or anyone else. I repent of all disobedience, rebellion, mistreatment of others, lying, cheating, using or slandering your name in vain. I repent on behalf of me and my entire bloodline of all perversion, lust, incest, fornication, adultery, idolatry, all witchcraft, murder, and any occult involvement.

Heavenly Father, I ask for Your forgiveness and cleansing through the blood of Your Son, the Lord Jesus Christ.

Lord Jesus, I now take the authority you have given me and ask that you anoint me now as I command all demonic spirits of religion, anger, rage, fear, depression, destruction, torment, guilt, bondage, vagabond, rejection, unforgiveness, bitterness, mind-control, double-mindedness, confusion, passivity, sickness, diseases, pain, fetter and all addictions to food, alcohol, drugs, sex, pornography, gambling, or nicotine to come out in the name of Jesus.

DELIVERANCE PRAYER

No demonic spirit is welcome in this holy temple now or every again!

I break all evil spoken curses and spells that may have been performed and/or spoken over my life and any evil curses resulting from involvement with Ouija board, psychics, tarot cards, horoscopes, secular music, or through TV, movies or pornography.

I break all evil curses off my family, marriage, children and relatives. I break every shackle, chain, cord, habit, craving, debt, soul-ties and any spirit that has tried to rob, kill, or destroy my life.

I command my entire family to be set free right now in the name of Jesus. I break every demonic assignment over my bloodline. Every evil entity, loose them now! In Jesus' name! According to Galatians 3:13, Christ has redeemed us from the curse of the law.

Jesus Christ is the only Way, the Truth, and the Life. I am now God's child and through my Lord Jesus Christ, I am able to cast down all demonic forces, powers and spirits that come against me or in my family's lives.

I am not cursed, but blessed! I am blessed coming in and blessed going out. I am above and not beneath. I am the head and not the tail. I am blessed and what God has blessed cannot be cursed. I am free, and I am saved. I have now exercised my faith and know that confession is made unto salvation (Romans 10:9,10). All of my sins have been remitted, and I am now forever loosed from the curse that came as a result of disobedience and rebellion to the Word of God.

Thank You Heavenly Father, thank you Lord Jesus, thank you Holy Spirit for forgiving me, guiding me and loving me unconditionaly. Thank you for setting me free from every form of bondage, every curse and evil spirit that has operated in my life. Father God, I pray for discernment and for a new vision to help me recognize and resist all evil and all fleshly, worldly desires. I am anointed through the Lord Jesus Christ, and I thank You Jesus for your guidance and discipline as I continue to be a victorious soldier and holy child of Yours to go and change the nations for Your glory's sake. I pray all this in Your Son's name Jesus Christ. AMEN.

Now go, and enjoy your new freedom journey.
Be Blessed.

I'd like to thank Bob Bassler & New Life Deliverance Center for these deliverance notes, which were modified and used with permission.

www.ingramcontent.com/pod-product-compliance
Lightning Source LLC
Chambersburg PA
CBHW061253120726
48001CB00001B/290